COVENANTS

God's way with his people

O. Palmer Robertson

GREAT COMMISSION
PUBLICATIONS

ISBN 0-934688-39-7

Printed 2003
DigiPrint, Inc.

Printed in USA

Published by
GREAT COMMISSION PUBLICATIONS
3640 Windsor Park Drive
Suwanee, GA 30024-3897
www.gcp.org

Great Commission Publications is the joint publishing
ministry of the Committee on Christian Education of the
Orthodox Presbyterian Church and the Committee for
Christian Education & Publications of the
Presbyterian Church in America.

Table of Contents

INTRODUCTION

Do you want something to keep you close to God? Something that will give you confidence that you are never without him? Then you're searching for God's covenant, his undying promise.

"I will be your God and you will be my people" is the heartbeat of every divine covenant in the Bible. This formula of hope appears in the first book of the Bible to reassure a man frustated with waiting (Gen. 17:7, 8). In the last book of the Bible it bursts with brilliance to illuminate the believer's final glory (Rev. 21:3). Between the beginning and the end, the constant encouragement of the man or woman needing God is that same covenantal center: God has committed himself so that he can be forever your God and you can be his people.

When you conclude that your personal world is falling apart, you may be reacting to the tensions of a marriage or the problems of a career. You may be perplexed over the search for purpose and a sense of hollowness in all your efforts and relationships.

God's covenants provide the foundation and structure for life. Marriage is best understood as a covenant, a three-way commitment between the man, the woman and the Lord. Parents and children can best relate to one another in their awareness of God's covenant with the family. Responsibilities at work derive meaning only from understanding the bond that God first made with the world at creation.

On the other hand, if you are thinking internationally, delving into questions about God's purposes for the nations, you still have to think in terms of God's covenants. Understanding his ancient bond with particular peoples is the only way to unravel the complex issues of twentieth-century politics.

So it's time to become absorbed with God's covenants, to *know* them in the Old Testament sense of becoming enmeshed in their reality.

This heartfelt knowledge will stabilize your personal life. It will sensitize your soul to a new awareness of God's agenda in the world. It will transform your family into the kind of nuclear unit that impacts the world.

1

THE COVENANT: A BOND IN BLOOD

"This was our first time to be surrounded by a group of angry cannibals, but God delivered us." (From an old missionary diary; Garlock, H. B. *Before We Kill and Eat You*, ed. Ruthanne Garlock. *Christ for the Nations*, Dallas, Tex., 1974: 75).

Five missionaries were surrounded by natives with cutlasses and spears, threatening to kill. A native boy had disappeared from the missionary school and the missionaries were being blamed. Since the natives were cannibals themselves they may have suspected that the missionaries had eaten the poor lad. That evening King Tho and his elders returned, begging the missionaries to overlook what they had done in anger. The child had returned on his own, safe and sound.

After the apology the throat of a white bird was cut. The blood was sprinkled first on the missionaries and then on the natives. The chief declared that a blood covenant had been made between the two parties. Never would they shed the blood of the missionaries and never would the missionaries shed the blood of the natives. All future generations on both sides of the covenant were committed by this ceremony.

Covenants Then and Now

Although occurring in a remote tribe of West Africa two thousand years after Bible times, the custom of these people duplicates almost exactly the ancient tradition of covenant-making procedures recorded in the Bible. Many times over God and people were bound together by the blood of the covenant.

Men and women today sign a contract to seal an agreement. If the issue merits it, the signing process may include the endorsement of a notary public to confirm the commitment. A notarized signature represents a legally binding oath that can be violated only with severe legal consequences.

Several different ceremonies underscore the solemnity of the various bonds God made with his people. Animal pieces were divided, sacrifice was offered, a meal was eaten, blood was sprinkled, the people passed under a shepherd's staff (cf Gen. 15:10, 18; 26:28-30; Ex. 24:8; Ezek. 20:37). Most of these ceremonies represented an oath-taking procedure. Formal oaths may not play such an important role in today's society, but the fact that God the Creator bound himself by covenant oaths is a significant reality to which Scripture repeatedly attests.

The seriousness of the divine oath is emphasized by the phraseology used to describe the way God makes a covenant. God "cuts" a covenant with men (cf Gen. 15:18; Ex. 24:8). Of course it is not the covenant itself that is cut. Instead the phrase refers to the animals that were cut as the ceremony of covenant-making was solemnized.

So What?

It may be a matter of social curiosity to note that primitive man cut animals to make a covenant while civilized man signs a contract. But what is the relevance for today of the more ancient practice? It's as relevant as the birth, marriage and obituary columns of the newspaper.

Death, for instance, comes because the covenant between God and man was violated. It may be convenient to believe that death results naturally because of man's humanity. But conscience and God's covenant confirm something else: because we have broken the binding oath of the covenant, death stalks us to the grave.

Jesus Christ confirmed the continuing significance of the bond of life and death embodied in God's covenants when he took the cup and said, "This cup is the new covenant in my blood, which is poured out for you" (Luke 22:20). Because he understood the deeper significance of God's covenant with man, Jesus pointed to the blood of the covenant.

Signs and Tokens

Throughout history God has given certain signs with his covenants. When a bride and groom pledge their loyalty to one another they exchange rings. These rings serve as token and pledge of their constant faith and abiding love.

God appointed the rainbow as the sign of his promise to Noah (Gen. 9:12-17). To confirm his covenant with Abraham he instituted circumcision (Gen. 17:9-14). In revealing his work to Moses God designated the Sabbath day as the everlasting sign between himself and Israel (Ex. 31:13). David was anointed as king both for himself and for his sons (Ps. 89:20, 29). In the new covenant, baptism and the covenant meal of the Lord's Supper were established by Jesus as signs of the unity he maintains with his people (Matt. 26:26-29; 28:18-20).

What's the worth of a sign? Nothing, nothing at all — unless the person giving the sign stands ready to back up its significance. If at an auction you give a signal that you are willing to pay $10,000 for a painting, you had better be ready to stand behind your raised hand: giving the sign commits you. You have bound yourself by oath to the auctioneers.

If you want certainty about what will or will not transpire in the world today, consider the signs of God's covenants. They stand as clear indicators of God's commitments to men and women. He has bound himself — and his people are bound to him — in a life-and-death oath by the signs of the covenant.

God Sets the Terms

One feature deserves special notice. The almighty Creator of all things doesn't leave the terms of his covenants to the whims and fancies of our imagination. The Lord in his own wisdom sets the boundaries of blessing and responsibility in his covenants.

Adam didn't say, "Lord, I like the freedom you've given me to eat from all these different kinds of trees. I'm even willing to do a little gardening here and there. But I won't agree to your proposals so long as you deny me the privilege of eating from the tree of the knowledge of good and evil." He didn't try to bargain with God, because he understood that divine covenants are sovereignly administered. The Lord alone sets the terms of his bonds with men. So may it ever be. God alone determines the bounds of the activities of his creation.

In sum: A covenant may be defined as *a bond in blood sovereignly administered.* Life and death are at stake in the divine covenants. God has bound himself to humans and them to himself. Life in your soul, blessing in your family, prosperity in your work and the course of the world—all these matters hinge on the provisions of God's covenants. Your personal peace (in the Hebrew sense of "total blessedness") will derive only from your walking and believing in the ways of his covenants.

11

Review Questions

1. How may a covenant be defined?

2. Can you think of concrete ways in which men today try to determine for themselves the terms of their relation to God and the world rather than acknowledging the authority of God in the covenant?

3. What are some of the signs God has used with his covenant?

Discussion Questions

1. How did you react when you read the story of King Tho and his elders?

2. What promise or agreement is described in these passages: Genesis 15:10, 18; Genesis 26:28-30; Exodus 24:8; Ezekiel 20:37?

3. How does Luke 22:20 fulfill the Old Testament covenants?

2

COVENANTAL BEGINNINGS

The Covenant of Creation

Are you an atheist? Do you find it difficult to convince yourself of the reality of God? If so you're like a fish who doesn't believe in the ocean.

The atheistic fish breaks the surface of the water. He shakes himself free of every last drop of brine. He boldly proclaims, "I don't believe in the ocean." Then he flops back into the water, catches his breath and starts his atheistic exercise all over again.

Most people know nothing about God's covenants. They may never have heard the word *covenant* in a theological context. But they are all covenant creatures. From the beginning of God's creational handiwork all have been bound in covenant with the Almighty.

They may not know this fact consciously, but they can't deny it deep down inside. They also know they are obligated to submit their wills to the will of the Creator. They even know they are covenant-breakers, worthy of death (Rom. 1:32). They are like the fish who tries to disbelieve the ocean.

God's Mold for Creation

At creation God bound mankind to himself in a covenant of life and death. He put Adam and Eve to the test. The tree of the knowledge of good and evil played a key role in this testing procedure: obedience meant life and disobedience meant death. In this original bond no provision was made for blessing in the event of their breaking the covenant. Adam needed to understand that, although he was a glorious creature, he was not a sovereign creature.

But let's not make the first man's existence seem confined to a single decision. Adam didn't stand idly beneath this one tree picking petals off daisies while chanting:

I will eat of the tree — I will not eat;
I will eat of the tree — I will not eat;
I will eat of the tree — I will not eat.

In addition to this special test, God constructed the world so that this unique image-bearer would have responsibilities consonant with his personal dignity as man. He must marry and multiply; he must subdue the earth; he must lead the world in its consecration of all things to the glory of God. Marriage, labor and Sabbath — these are the creation ordinances which belong to the fabric of the universe. Like the law of gravity, these ordinances stabilize the world God made.

In the little industrial center of Anniston, Alabama, mighty presses turn steel plates into fixed, functional metal shapes. After the plates are heated to a temperature that makes them malleable, massive machines exert pressures of approximately six thousand tons — that's 12,000,000 pounds — to conform them to a chosen mold.

God's ordinances of creation shape the world as those mighty presses form the steel. Far from functioning as polite options to which a person may or may not conform, these laws of creational reality define the state of things. Transgress at your own risk!

Consider these basic elements of God's covenantal structure with the original man.

First, the Sabbath. The Sabbath is a good point to begin this discussion of God's creation mandates because we are prone to resist any structure that would dictate the form of our personal worship. Because of this quest for absolute freedom in worship, it becomes all the more necessary to note that from the beginning it was not so.

God blessed and sanctified the Sabbath day (Gen. 2:3). This blessing, this sanctifying, was not a word uttered into a vacuum. It *did* something. It affected the rudiments of the universe on a level that compares to the basic structure of matter. Particularly for the sake of men and women, God blessed and sanctified the Sabbath. As the Lord of the Sabbath himself said, "The Sabbath was made for man" (Mark 2:27).

Yes, Christ argued about Sabbath rules. His controversy, however, was not with the ordinance of creation as reported in the early verses of Genesis: it was with picky rules of the self-appointed Sabbath technicians of his day. But neither he nor his disciples, either by word or by example, contradicted the principle that we need a regular day for stirring the fires of our consecration to God.

Cold glass will shatter under the slightest pressure attempting to alter its shape. But heated red-hot and placed in the hands of the artisan, it may be molded merely by breath or touch. So men and women need the fires of their devotion kindled regularly. Then they may be molded according to the will of their Creator. Just as much today as in the first hours of their creation, the weekly ordinance by which men and women preserve their priorities must be maintained.

Second, marriage. The time has certainly come to stress the creation origins of the marriage institution — not because of possible tax advantages but because the sexual realm must manifest the separateness of a holy consecration: two and only two will be one flesh (Gen. 2:18; cf Mark 10:7, 8).

An ordinance of God as old as this world but as fresh as each new day ought to be heard and heeded by the young of today: (1) get married; (2) have children; (3) raise those children in the nurture and admonition of the Lord. When thrashing about trying to find purpose and meaning, goals and callings in life, get back to the basics! (1) Get married; (2) have children; (3) raise those children in the Lord. Some of the most essential reasons for existence center on those basic principles.

Paul's "It is good for a man not to marry" (1 Cor. 7:1) harmonizes with the divine declaration at creation: "It is not good for the man to be alone" (Gen. 2:18). Because of the distresses of the present hour, and by reason of a special gift, some men and women will serve God and humans most usefully and joyfully in a single state. Yet their distinctive situation must not detract from the creation ordinance. Marriage ought to be viewed as the course that ordinarily should be followed, while life in an unmarried situation may be a God-appointed but extraordinary circumstance.

A careful review of the original structure of marriage points to the way by which some of the modern fears and misapprehensions about marriage can be relieved. Scripture declares that God made for man a "helper suitable for him" (Gen. 2:18). The original language of the Bible uses only two words: *helper* and *suitable for him*. These two elements provide the kind of balance necessary to keep the loveboat of marriage on an even keel.

Scripture as well as nature indicates that the woman was made for the man and not *vice versa* (1 Cor. 11:9). The battle of the sexes will be unending unless this basic principle is perceived. The woman finds fulfillment as she functions as helper to the man.

Balancing this principle is the other dimension of the creation order. The woman is a helper "corresponding to" the man. In every way she is the image of God just as he. Her dignity as a person in no way is beneath his. If she is to be helper to the man, her appointed calling can be realized only as she realizes her fullest potential as a person equally made after the likeness of God's glory. Only as her gifts and abilities reach their greatest maturity can she provide the help her husband will need.

The man in turn exercises leadership in a way that guarantees that she reaches her full potential. Not as a swellhead or a hothead but as a saving, loving head does the man manifest the wisdom of God in the bonds of marriage (Eph. 5:22-28). He functions as a lover, lavishing self-sacrificing care on the one to whom he is wed.

Third, labor. The third ordinance of creation that will provide a return of fullness of life when observed is the command to subdue the earth (Gen. 1:28). Though stated in a single little phrase, this command possesses cosmic implications. Harnessing the power of the atom as well as harvesting the potential of outer space receives its justification from this first directive from on high.

Manual labor derives its dignity from this command to subdue the earth. Imagine Uzziah, one of Israel's greatest kings, out in the field working with a hoe, crunching dirt clods between his hands — and enjoying every minute of it! He loved the soil (2 Chron. 26:10).

Contrary to the modern ideal of escaping work, the Bible presumes labor will be performed with well-defined constancy. The principle of the Sabbath assumes that six days of labor will be associated with the one day of rest. Not necessarily on the job or at the office but one way or another men and women should set themselves to the tasks before them with a patterned order. Whether programming for a computer, beautifying the lawn or sanding the rust spots off your old auto, work ought to be done with reverence and regularity.

The New Testament makes it quite plain that work is not optional. Even in the context of new-covenant grace, good hard work remains essential:

> For you yourselves know how you ought to follow our example. We were not idle when we were with you, nor did we eat anyone's food without paying for it. On the contrary, we worked night and day, laboring and toiling so that we would not be a burden to any of you. We did this, not because we do not have the right to such help, but in order to make ourselves a model for you to follow. For even when we were with you, we gave you this rule: "If a man will not work, he shall not eat" (2 Thess. 3:7-10).

These creational ordinances of the Sabbath, marriage and labor contain the divine formula for right relationships in God's world. To violate any of these principles is to fly in the face of reality. The fact that modern men and women so glibly question each of these principles indicates just how far they have drifted into the abysmal state of meaningless relativity.

Radical Obedience

The focal point in this covenant of creation has not yet been touched on. Life ultimately hinges on our readiness to hear and to heed the voice of God simply because it *is* God's voice.

The justification for finding the life-principle in submission to the word of God is displayed vividly in the ultimate test of the original man's readiness to obey God's word simply because God said so. Adam might have reasoned that he ought to toil in the ground, replenish the earth and consecrate all to God. But only the raw word of God could have indicated to him that he must not eat from one particular tree of the garden though he had free access to all the others.

Was Adam willing to bring his will under the authority of God? Would he give full recognition to the fact that God the Creator stood infinitely above man the creature? Only if he acknowledged that the source of life existed in a Person outside himself could he continue to live.

Centuries later the ultra-drama of Gethsemane focused in a similar fashion on the radical obedience of the Son of God. In his hours of testing Jesus achieved the submission to the will of God that was essential for our salvation. Although *never* disobedient, he learned obedience on its deepest level of intensity (see Heb. 5:8). In successive stages he moved from

[I]f it is possible, may this cup be taken from me (Matt. 26:39)

to

[I]f it is not possible for this cup to be taken away unless I drink it, may your will be done (Matt. 26:42)

to

Shall I not drink the cup the Father has given me? (John 18:11).

The first man failed the test and in his failure he lost life. By his action he also forfeited all claim to life for subsequent generations. In the original bond between God and man no provision for blessing had been offered in the event of disobedience. As a result, in Adam all die (1 Cor. 15:22). By the one disobedience of the one man the many were made sinners (Rom. 5:19). The goodness of God in the creation of mankind was repudiated for a hollow autonomy that sentenced man to die alone.

Review Questions

1. What are the three creational ordinances and what spheres of life do they affect?

2. What contemporary problems in the areas of worship, marriage and work would be addressed by a fuller understanding of the creation ordinances?

Discussion Questions

1. Which aspects of your marriage, work or worship are ready for growth or need correction now?

2. What particular problems will you meet if you seek to change your life-patterns in these areas?

3. How does your family strengthen its covenantal bond with God on Sunday?

4. How would you help a person who must work on Sunday because of necessity or mercy fulfill his need for worship and rest?

3

PUTTING UP THE BOND

Adam: The Covenant of Commencement

The time for final trial and sentence had not yet come. But the man was unquestionably guilty.

What to do with him?

Incarceration would serve no good purpose. Since the ultimate intent of this Judge was to satisfy justice some other way than by giving the lawbreaker his just deserts, an immediate infliction of the death penalty would contradict this gracious purpose.

So the supreme Authority chastened the rebellious for his own good, sent him on his way, and bound himself by a most solemn promise that justice will be maintained even as the undeserved gift of life is bestowed.

When a person accused of a serious crime is freed until trial, a bond may be set. In the case currently under consideration no higher bond could be conceived of than the solemn oath of the God of the covenant. If the Lord did not come through with all he promised, his integrity as God would be shattered forever.

A Promise Made

The parallels between God's treatment of man after sin and a modern law-system's treatment of a criminal cannot be pressed in every detail; yet the basic idea of God's putting up bond in the form of a covenant commitment certainly is apropos.

God had absolutely no obligation to man once he had revolted against the Almighty's will and aligned himself with the serpent, who is Satan. How presumptuous people are today, thinking that God owes them a living, that some oughtness dictates their right to good health, prosperity and plenty. Nothing could be further from the truth! You may not see every sin as a Satanically inspired rebellion deserving death; but your insensitivity to sin's heinousness cannot nullify the reality of the fact that by sin you have forfeited every claim to life and its blessings.

But God is gracious — he bound himself by oath. Although man proved to be an ungrateful, self-willed rebel, God chose to obligate himself to the sinner. Read the commitment of the Creator as found in Genesis 3:14-19.

First: "I will put enmity between you [Satan] and the woman." Note that this enmity is God-initiated. Otherwise the man and the woman would have remained united with Satan in his opposition to God.

Second: God will also put enmity "between your [Satan's] offspring and hers [the woman's]." Now the enmity, still initiated by God, is depicted as though it were surging from two armed camps. A multiple of each seed will engage in mortal conflict. Down through the long corridors of time this struggle will continue.

Third: "[H]e [of the woman] will crush your [Satan's] head, and you [Satan] will strike his heel." Now the conflict returns to a hand to hand combat between two individuals, one representing all the hardened host of Satan, the other representing the redeemed host of God.

Fourth: The woman shall give birth, but only in a context of great pain and sorrow.

Fifth: The man shall eat life-sustaining bread, but only as a result of excessive labor for the fruit produced.

Sixth: In the end humans made of dust shall return to the dust.

Those who are inclined to half-believe the Bible prefer to view this narrative as a myth, a legend, a saga. It explains for them the basic struggles of primitive man. Snakes strike at the heel and men retaliate. But honestly, isn't the setting of the struggle in Genesis itself much deeper? Even if these words do explain animosity between snakes and men they also depict a deeper hatred between God and the Tempter, a struggle into which man and woman inevitably were drawn.

Consider the basic insights into life that are crammed into these brief words. Providing bread, relieving pain, performing labor, bearing children and dealing with the inevitability of death — these are the certain issues that none can escape. All of these concerns receive recognition in these brief verses.

A Saving Hero

But ultimately into the arena of human history one single saving hero will enter. As a representative man like Adam, this hero will engage Satan himself in mortal conflict. While Satan will strike this one Man's heel, the one Man will crush Satan's head. These verses anticipate precisely the life and death of Jesus Christ, the ultimate Man. He "disarmed the [Satanic] powers and authorities . . . [and] made a public spectacle of them, triumphing over them by the cross" (Col. 2:15).

Satan thought he had crushed the Christ — he nailed him to the cross! With every blow of the hammer he thought he was finishing the job. But in that very cross Satan was defeated, his power broken. His captive hold on the sinner was ruined by his own ruthless cleverness.

The condemning power inherent in sin worked its worst on the innocent Son of God. The appointed Seed of the woman suffered sin's consequences in place of the sinner. As the Lord had promised when he initiated the covenant, the crushing of the appointed Man would substitute for the wounding of the sinner.

Between these two great archetypical men — between Adam and Christ — the long history of the two seeds unfolds. Because he "belonged to the evil one" Cain killed his brother in a jealous rage (Gen. 4:8; 1 John 3:12). But Enoch "walked with God; then he was no more, because God took him away" (Gen. 5:24). Later Goliath stands out as a representative man, challenging the people of God to a contest to the death. "Choose a man," he exclaims, "and have him come down to me. If he is able to fight and kill me, we will become your subjects; but if I overcome him and kill him, you will become our subjects and serve us" (cf 1 Sam. 17:8, 9). So David the anointed of the Lord takes up the challenge and destroys the seed of Satan. By faith in the God who was on his side he slew the giant with Goliath's own sword.

The contemporary significance of this same struggle is seen in the natural alignment of all humans on Satan's side. As for you, "you followed the ways . . . of the ruler of the kingdom of the air, the spirit who is now at work in those who are disobedient" (Eph. 2:2). By nature all are of this seed of Satan, but the grace of God sets up an animosity against Satan within the hearts of men and women. This work of God's Spirit continues today, fulfilling the original design of God's covenant.

The covenant commitment of God to work animosity against Satan in the hearts of particular men and women despite their natural alignment with the cause of Satan is summarized in Genesis 3. Only in seed form but promising extensive fruit over the ages, this covenant commitment of the Lord explains the pattern of the lives of people today whether Christian or non-Christian. Everyone struggles with the problems and pains associated with labor, sickness, birth, death, marriage and community. But on the deeper level the struggle revolves about loyalties to Satan or to God. Ultimately it centers on the life-and-death struggle between Satan and the Christ which climaxed at the cross of Calvary.

Review Questions

1. Trace some of the steps in the unfolding of the two seeds mentioned in Genesis 3:15.

2. What changes in the order of the world does God institute in Genesis 3:14-18?

Discussion Questions

1. What are some of the characteristics that mark the behavior of a person who is of the seed of Satan?

2. How is the struggle between the two seeds reflected in your neighborhood or at work? in world events?

3. What is the greatest practical hindrance you face in manifesting the characteristics of the seed of God in your marriage or at work?

4. What steps can you take to begin to overcome this hindrance?

4

PRESERVATION FOR SALVATION

Noah: The Covenant of Preservation

Right in the middle of the development of the two seeds God established a covenant with Noah. As the floodwaters rose to swallow unrepentant sinners they simultaneously lifted the ark bearing Noah and his family to safety.

God had said that a great struggle between the seeds would develop. Centuries later Jesus Christ would talk about wheat and tares growing together in the field of the world. Seed would struggle against seed for survival (Matt. 13:24-30).

Two Seeds

The first son of Adam had murder in his heart. He killed his brother in a fit of jealousy (Gen. 4:8). He displayed his nature as the seed of the evil one (1 John 3:12). Then Lamech took two wives, murdered a man and shouted defiantly against God and anyone else who might attempt an act of vengeance against him (Gen. 4:23, 24). Then there was Babel, an early metropolis seeking to unify everyone in rebellion. Because God told them to scatter across the face of the earth, they determined to band together in one place. There together they could build a tower to heaven as a symbol of their self-unification and self-deification (Gen. 11:4).

The seed of Satan. Resistant and recalcitrant. Reproducing itself. Threatening to overrun the universe. Degenerate to the core.

On the other side: *the seed of the woman.* A product of God's intervening grace, this line leads to Christ. God himself maintained this seed against all odds. Seth, whose name means "set," was set by God in the place of his murdered brother (Gen. 4:25). The seed was preserved.

Enoch walked with God, an amazing feat indeed! He maintained close, intimate, personal fellowship with the Creator. While the world was burning about him he walked with God; and when he was not, he *was not*, for God took him. Body and spirit alike were gone because they both were God's (Gen. 5:24; cf Heb. 11:5).

Another Lamech represented the seed of the woman, a product of God's grace among a fallen humanity. He had his hard times, his struggles in search of rainbows in a fallen world. But Lamech had hope in the word of God. Straining to eke out an existence, he named his son "Rest" (the meaning of *Noah*). In his mind this son might be the promised seed — the one to give relief from the curse of burdensome toil to which the world had been condemned (Gen. 5:28, 29).

In the midst of the early development of the two seeds Noah and his generation arise. On the one hand, the degeneracy of the seed of Satan is extensive in Noah's day. On the other hand, the working of God's favor in the life of Noah and his family displays God's determination to continue his work of salvation until a new world bathed by the righteous judgments of God has been born.

Emphases of the Covenant with Noah

Consider a few of the basic emphases that arise in God's covenant with Noah. Observe how they stretch even into the present era of God's dealings with men.

1. Notice the *interconnection* between God's covenant with Noah and his previous covenantal commitments. Although the term *covenant* now appears for the first time in the Bible the complex of ideas behind the covenant concept are by no means new. Redemption is as broad as creation and includes all the facets of man's relation to the world.

After they sinned Adam and Eve still had the same obligations to God and his world as before the fall. So that there can be no mistake, Noah is told explicitly to be fruitful and increase in number (Gen. 9:1). The blessings and obligations of the marriage relationship continue unbroken.

In similar fashion it is stated that the fear and dread of man will fall on all creation (Gen. 9:2). Something has gone wrong — the harmonious relationship between humans and the environment has been disturbed. A note of dissonance reverberates. Yet the echo of the original command to subdue the earth (Gen. 1:26) is present in these words. In the realm of labor we have a continuing responsibility despite the distortions of sin.

No explicit mention is made in God's covenant with Noah concerning the Sabbath, although the constancy of a regulated pattern of labor implies also a regulation of rest. The broader patterns of the Sabbath and redemption are also found in the hope of Noah's father—he looks for rest and memorializes his dream by naming his son Noah (Rest). He expects relief from the relentless struggle against a cursed creation. These broader implications of the Sabbath pattern appear in God's covenant with Noah.

Despite the grind of labor and the tensions of marriage, both these institutions must be viewed today from a covenantal perspective. Not awkward, unneeded appendices to the spiritual life, these elements contribute to the wholeness of man's relation to God. Their reiteration in the covenant with Noah shows their continuing importance.

2. The *particularity* of God's redemptive grace is demonstrated in the covenant with Noah. You may not understand it. You may not even like what you understand, but you must accept it as true. From the mass of depraved humanity God shows grace toward Noah and his family. They experience the blessings of salvation while others continue in their hardened ways.

The depths to which men and women had sunk are clearly described in the book of Genesis. God saw that their wickedness was great — so great that every imagination of the thoughts of mankind's heart was only evil all the time (Gen. 6:5). The first impulse, the formative framework for man's every thought, was exclusively evil.

But Noah found grace in God's eyes. Toward this particular man among the mass of undeserving humanity

God showed the richness of his unmerited favor. That's the meaning of grace: unmerited and undeserved blessing.

This grace may have kept Noah from sinking to the levels of debauchery found among his contemporaries; but it nonetheless was grace undeserved by the man himself. Noah did not find favor in the eyes of the Lord (Gen. 6:8) because he was a righteous man (Gen. 6:9). No, the structure of the book of Genesis speaks against this kind of causal connection between Genesis 6:9 and 6:8. The phrase *these are the generations of* which begins Genesis 6:9 is a formalized sectional heading that begins each of ten different portions of the book of Genesis, and it effectively places Genesis 6:9 in a section separate from the assertion of Genesis 6:8. Noah found grace because grace is *grace*, not because of goodness inherent in Noah. Grace alone singles out this particular man to make him the object of God's favor.

3. Observe the emphasis on *God's dealing with families* in the covenant of redemption. God likes to save individuals, men and women, boys and girls, from sin and judgment; but central to the heart of God is the reconstitution of families. Grace in the covenant extends toward the whole of the family.

Over and over God indicates his commitment to deal with Noah and his entire house by bringing them into the ark of salvation. "You and your sons and your wife and your sons' wives with you" becomes a repeated theme characteristic of this covenant (cf Gen. 6:18; 7:1, 7, 13, 23; 8:16, 18; 9:9, 12). Noah is set apart as the head of the family for a unique position in the eyes of God.

Look closely at the text of Scripture: "The LORD then said to Noah, 'Go into the ark, you and your whole family, because I have found you righteous in this generation' " (Gen. 7:1). This "you" is singular and refers to Noah alone. Because the head of the house was found righteous all his house was to go into the ark. It was by faith that Noah "built an ark to save his family" and so became an heir of the righteousness of faith (Heb. 11:7).

God delights in saving families. The basic structure of creation's order finds its counterpart in redemption. This point of covenant order needs special recognition in view of the intense individualism that characterizes western society today. Think about it.

4. Note the concentration on *preservation* found in this covenant. God commits himself to preserve the present order of the world so that the work of redemption may be accomplished. Seedtime and harvest, cold and heat, summer and winter, day and night will never cease as long as the earth endures (Gen. 8:22). The world will be kept free of massive disturbances like Noah's flood. Instead regularity and order will preserve the human race and the environment.

The institution by God of the first inklings of human self-government in this covenant with Noah supports the theme of preservation. For as mankind began to expand rapidly across the face of the earth God instituted human government as a way of restraining the self-destructive principles within society.

Prior to this point God had restricted to himself alone the taking of a human life. No one but God must touch

Cain for his fratricide (Gen. 4:15). But now as a means of restraining mankind God entrusts the administration of justice to humans. Note the poetic parallelism that heightens the significance of this moment in God's dealing with mankind:

> a He who sheds
> b the blood of
> c man;
> c by man
> b his blood
> a shall be shed.
>
> Genesis 9:6

Far from being simply a statement of fact describing how things will inevitably fall out, this verse explains precisely how God will demand an accounting of the manslayer, whether he be human or beast (Gen. 9:5). Mankind becomes God's appointed instrument for the execution of the murderer.

Modern sociologists may debate the deterrent value of capital punishment and in different decades arrive at differing conclusions. Yet the covenant with Noah indicates that capital punishment will serve in the place of God's own actions of temporal vengeance. As such it will have the effect of establishing a self-restraining influence on human society. The earth will be preserved by the restraints placed on our self-destructive tendencies.

These self-restraining principles in the covenant with Noah are expanded in the later legislation of the Mosaic covenant. Whether animal or human, the murderous creature's life must be taken (Ex. 21:28; 21:12; Num. 35:16-21).

In the new covenant this same principle is restated. The state is a servant of God, instilling terror in the heart of the evildoer. Its power is the sword by which it executes vengeance on the wicked (Rom. 13:1-5; 1 Pet. 2:13, 14).

God's purposes are always good. The steady stream of abuse of power by the state must not detract from the basic principle. God's purpose in the covenant with Noah was to preserve the earth until today. A vital part of that covenant is the obligation belonging to those in authority whether they recognize it or not.

5. A *universalistic dimension* of the Noahic covenant balances the particular choices of God's grace treated earlier. This covenant with Noah embraces the whole of creation: every living creature benefits from its blessings (Gen. 9:10).

The universalistic dimension of God's covenant with Noah tells you what to expect in the future. It is not that every single soul will be saved in the end. The destruction of the wicked by Noah's floodwaters makes that point quite plain. But the fallen universe can expect complete reconstitution in a day that is coming soon.

Inanimate creation as a whole will benefit from the redemption of men and women. As the apostle Paul says, "The creation waits in eager expectation for the sons of God to be revealed. For the creation . . . itself will be liberated from its bondage to decay and brought into the glorious freedom of the children of God" (Rom. 8:19-21). At the resurrection of the bodies of believers in Jesus Christ the earth itself will undergo a drastic change. Through human sin the creation fell under God's curse, and by

God's blessing the creation will be renewed at the resurrection.

The universalistic dimension of God's covenant with Noah also has implications for proclaiming the good news today. Psalm 19 celebrates the regularity of sun and moon, of day and night, as a way by which God's grace to the world is proclaimed throughout the earth. "Day unto day they pour forth speech, night after night they display knowledge" (Ps. 19:2). Although their "voice" is not heard their "[body] language" has gone out to the ends of the earth. Because of the regularity of day and night as established in the covenant with Noah all men and women receive testimony of the grace of God.

This universal testimony provides the foundation for worldwide proclamation of the gospel. Because God has commissioned day and night and sun and moon to proclaim the message of his grace everywhere, a foundation has been laid for the universal proclamation of the gospel of Jesus Christ. Everyone everywhere ought to hear. The Gentiles ought to hear, since both Moses and Isaiah prophesied of the salvation of those who never sought God (cf Rom. 10:19, 20). Furthermore even a dispersed Israel scattered across the face of the world by the judgment of God — even they ought to hear the saving gospel of Jesus Christ (cf Rom. 10:18, quoting Psalm 19).

6. Admire the *gracious character* of this covenant with Noah. Bloated rain clouds forebode destruction and devastation, but arching above the clouds is the colorful rainbow. It is God's bow, his token of mercy in the midst of the just condemnation of a godless humanity. Not surprisingly the rainbow reappears at the end of the Bible. In

the book of Revelation a rainbow arches over the throne of God (Rev. 4:3). Glittering like an emerald, it reminds of God's grace toward corrupted men and women. From beginning to end grace has endured, sustaining and finally saving sinners.

Believers in Christ may take comfort in the rainbow above the judgment-throne of God. By that symbol they are assured of the never-failing grace of the unchanging covenant-maker. Thousands of years ago he made a covenant with Noah; for eternity he remains faithful to that covenant.

Review Questions

1. Trace the development of the two seeds from Adam to Noah.

2. What are the six emphases of the covenant with Noah?

Discussion Questions

1. How do some elements of the covenant with Noah provide encouragement to you? How do others provide warning?

2. Write out how these warnings and encouragements will help you to grow or change this week, and possibly share them with someone.

5

"I PROMISE UNTO DEATH"

Abraham: The Covenant of Promise

It had been years since the Lord God appeared to Abraham. During all this time the patriarch's faith had been tested severely. God had promised Abraham a land flowing with milk and honey, yet he possessed not one single inch of the designated territory. God had promised Abraham that he would be a blessing to all the nations, but great plagues came on the Egyptians because of Abraham's deceitfulness. All the wombs of the household of Abimelech king of Gerar were shut up because of Sarah, Abraham's wife. Is that what should be called being a blessing to the nations? God had promised Abraham that his offspring would be as numerous as the sand on the seashore, yet he had not one single child to claim as his own.

Land and a Son

None of these promised blessings for Abraham can be appreciated apart from God's plan to save sinners from all nations. The idea of a promised land solidified the hope of a return to paradise. God wasn't interested merely in Middle Eastern real estate — he wanted men and women to hope for fullness of life!

When Abraham believed God about a supernaturally provided son (Gen. 15:6) it meant that Abraham was expecting his offspring to include the promised seed of Genesis 3:15 who would crush the head of Satan and deliver men and women from the curse of sin. Just as Noah's father Lamech had hoped that his son would be the one to deliver them from the curse of the ground (Gen. 5:28) so Abraham now hoped that his son would be the one through whom the blessing of God would flow. How else could he understand the promise that in him all the nations of the earth would be blessed?

How Can I Know?

But how could Abraham *know*? What basis for assurance did he have? Nothing in his life-experience encouraged the expectation of the fulfillment of God's promises. The Christian today also may have serious problems about assurance. If God has promised a godly seed, do you always see that promise fulfilled in your children? If God has promised blessing on your work, why do you wrestle so constantly with the sense of purpose in your life? If new life in Christ means victory over temptation, why do you experience so many backslidings into sin?

When God finally appeared again to Abraham the patriarch virtually pounced at his opportunity. "[H]ow can I know that I will gain possession of [the promise]?" was his plea (cf Gen. 15:8). The Lord answered in a most mysterious way — at least so far as modern customs are concerned. But Abraham understood from the start. Following the procedures of the day he divided several animals, placing the bloody pieces over against one another. Then he stood as solemn witness while a flaming torch and smoking furnace passed between the pieces. "On that day," says the Scripture, "the LORD made a covenant" with Abraham (Gen. 15:18).

What is the meaning of this strange procedure? How could it satisfy the yearning for assurance in Abraham's heart?

The Lord was offering the deepest possible assurance by making use of the customary covenant-making procedure of the day. The cutting of animals and the passing between the pieces bound the Lord himself by a most solemn oath. "May I be cut in pieces just as these animals have been mutilated if I fail to fulfill my promises," the ancient procedure proclaimed.

Archaeology provides illuminating parallels to this ritual. According to a text from the ancient kingdom of Babylon, men expressed curses on themselves as they performed a ritual of cutting animals:

> This head is not the head of the goat . . . it is the head of Mati'-ilu . . . If Mati'-ilu [breaks] this oath, as the head of this goat is cut off . . . so will the head of Mati'-ilu be cut off (cited in Leon Morris, *The Apostolic Preaching of the Cross*, 1956: 64).

How amazing — Almighty God committing himself in such a manner to a mere mortal! God could have sworn by the sun or the sea, he could have sworn by all the gold or precious jewels in all the secret caches of the earth; but none of these glamorous items could compare with the very essence of God himself. Since there was no greater than himself, he swore by himself. By solemn ceremony he pledged himself to death if he violated a single promise made to the patriarch.

Some 1400 years after the events of Genesis 15 the pledge-to-death of the covenant-making ceremony appears once more. King Nebuchadnezzar of Babylon knocks at Jerusalem's gate—only the king has not come to make a polite social call. He knocks with battering rams, determined to subjugate the little nation of Judah.

Judah's King Zedekiah had been certain that things could never come to this. "This is the temple of the LORD, the temple of the LORD, the temple of the LORD" was his chant of confidence (cf Jer. 7:4). How could the dwelling place of God be threatened by the armies of a heathen king? But Zedekiah was forced into reassessment. Perhaps his people had neglected the duties on their side of the covenant. Perhaps they had broken the law of their God and needed to make amends.

Through public reading of the law of the covenant it immediately became clear that the people had neglected the very first of Israel's statutory laws. They had failed to release their fellow-Israelite slaves at the end of the prescribed seven-year period (cf Ex. 21:1, 2). So King Zedekiah issued a decree that all Israelite slaves must be freed at once. The nobles of the land complied, but not for long. For the wives of the nobles were not accustomed to hard labor. They could not abide beating their own clothes and hauling their own water, so they insisted on enforcing servitude once more.

At this point the prophet spoke. He declared to the people the consequences of their violating the covenant:

The men who have violated my covenant and have not fulfilled the terms of the covenant they made before me, I will treat like the calf they cut in two and then walked between its pieces. The leaders of Judah and Jerusalem, the court officials, the priests and all the people of the land who walked between the pieces of the calf, I will hand over to their enemies who seek their lives. Their dead bodies will become food for the birds of the air and the beasts of the earth (Jer. 34:18-20).

Animals divided, people passing between the pieces, birds of prey devouring the cursed carcasses — the connection with Abraham's ancient vision is clear. Although occurring 1400 years after Abraham, the images are identical. By violating the pledge of the inauguration ceremony of the covenant the people of Israel have exposed themselves to awesome condemnations.

The vengeance of the covenant was swift. King Zedekiah fled from Nebuchadnezzar's siege through a crack in the city wall only to be overtaken by the Babylonian monarch. Nebuchadnezzar slaughtered the king's sons in his presence and then gouged out Zedekiah's eyes. The death of his own sons was etched into his memory as the last sight he ever witnessed. God judges covenantal infidelity with great severity. His righteous law *will* be maintained. The entire history of Israel's experience under the covenant testifies to that fact.

Covenant, Not Testament

God's action in bringing both blessing and judgment according to his covenant does not terminate with the Old Testament. As a matter of fact, only the New Testament fully shows God's consistency in acting according to the terms of the covenant. Two passages from the New Testament clearly display the continuing covenantal orientation of the Scriptures: Hebrews 9:15-20 and Luke 22:19, 20.

Because of the distinctiveness of its wording, Hebrews 9:17 is rarely translated so that its original significance is clear. Literally the verse reads, "For a covenant is made firm over dead bodies." Most translations favor understanding the verse as referring to a last will and testament, and undoubtedly this interpretation has much to support it.

But the context of these verses clearly speaks of a covenant inauguration ceremony, not of a testamentary disposition. The words make best sense in light of the ancient covenant-making ceremony of Abraham's day. In the passing between the mutilated pieces the covenant was inaugurated by the shedding of blood, symbolizing that the covenant-makers were pledged to death in the event of transgression. The covenant was not complete without this initial pledge to life *and* death at the inauguration. That's why Hebrews 9:17 states, "A covenant is made firm over dead bodies; for a covenant is not in effect so long as the covenant-maker lives." Without the symbolic representation of the death of the covenant-maker the covenant has not been sealed with the oath necessary for its validation. Just as a contract today is not binding until sealed by signatures, so a covenant of old was not in effect until sealed by the symbolic death of the covenant-maker. The covenant then became binding and any transgression resulted in death.

Provision for the possibility of substitution is distinctive to God's covenants in the Bible. Because of this element one party's death could substitute for another's. The covenant transgressor might not have to die if the terms of the covenant included the possibility of substitution.

No place may be found in the idea of a last will and testament for substituting someone else's death in place of the testator's. The one who makes a last will and testament must himself die before the will is activated. But in the framework of the covenant, Christ could die to set men and women free from the curses belonging to them as a result of their transgressing the Mosaic covenant. That is the central point of the Hebrews passage. Christ dies for others as a consequence of their covenantal violation, since "without the shedding of blood there is no forgiveness" (Heb. 9:22).

A second New Testament passage referring to covenant inauguration is found in Luke 22:19, 20. In the midst of the Passover celebration Jesus declares the word of new-covenant inauguration. Holding in his hand the dark-red wine of the Passover cup he speaks of a bond in blood, the blood of the new covenant poured out in substitution for many. The Passover meal of the old covenant was a celebration of deliverance from death and enslavement. Safe because of the blood of the lamb sprinkled on their doorposts, Israel in Egypt fellowshipped together and with their God through the ritual of the Passover. The cup of wine crystallized their moment of joy over the faithfulness of the God of Abraham to his covenant oath concerning their freedom to possess the land of promise.

On the night before his bloodshedding Jesus places his death directly in the stream of covenantal bloodshedding that had run through the ages. His blood was covenantal blood. His death was like the Passover lamb's death. An innocent individual would suffer death for guilty·covenant-breakers.

Behind the blood of the Mosaic Passover lamb lay the bloody pieces that formed the path for covenant consecration in Abraham's day. Abraham saw the flaming torch and smoking firepot passing between the pieces of divided animals. By this symbolism God passed between the pieces. By a most solemn oath he had committed himself to be true to his word. The lonely patriarch could "know for certain" (Gen. 15:13) that his seed would possess the land. He could know beyond the shadow of a doubt because God ran the bloody gauntlet.

At the end of that gauntlet was a form that has become most familiar to us today. It is the form of the cross of the Lord Jesus Christ. God pledged himself to death if it should be necessary for the fulfillment of his promises. Abraham could be assured because the Lord had taken an oath of self-malediction. Christ died on the cross because his substitutionary death provided the only way for God's word to prove true. By no other method could sinners be saved. If he did not die, all sinners would die. None could possess the promises.

At the fall of man God had committed himself to raise up a seed of the woman to crush the head of Satan, the serpent. Even as Satan struck his blow against the man, so the Man appointed would crush Satan and his power. At the cross of Christ Satan did his worst. He struck out with all his might against the Son of God. But by his attack against pure innocence Satan only destroyed himself. The sufferings of the Son of God substituted for the death deserved by covenant-breakers of all the ages.

Returning once more to the ancient vision of Abraham, a final question may be posed: Who passed between the pieces? Who ran the bloody gauntlet? *Only God passed between the pieces* — Abraham did not. *Only God* made the pledge-to-death of the covenant.

No wonder the patriarch could be perfectly certain of his blessings. The Lord God assumed to himself the obligations of *both* parties in the covenant. Whether God *or* Abraham broke the covenant — no matter! In either case the Lord would absorb into himself the curses of the covenant. Malediction was spoken only over the Lord himself.

So Christ came. He kept all the laws of the covenant. He lived in perfect harmony with every stipulation of the covenant. Yet he died. He underwent the curses of the covenant. Now he stands to offer the fullest blessings of life to the covenant-breakers who deserve death. "Take, eat," he says. "This is my body, broken for you." And the cup? "This is my blood of the new covenant poured out for many for the remission of sins." You come, you drink —all of you drink of it.

Dramatize your participation in the blessing of his sacrifice. Enjoy the confidence of ancient Abraham. Be assured of your eternal salvation through the blood of the everlasting covenant.

Review Questions

1. How did God confirm the covenant with Abraham?
2. What does it mean to "cut a covenant"?
3. How does the death of Jesus fulfill this event/ceremony?

Discussion Questions

1. How does a person become assured that God's love has provided a way of salvation for him?
2. How have you resolved the question of assurance in your own life? What barriers do people find in seeking assurance?
3. How is the Lord's Supper designed to assure you of the redemptive character of God's love for you?

6

A SEAL FOR THE PROMISE

A down payment—a notarized signature—a handshake —a kiss. Any of these actions may seal a promise. A man is as good as his word, but it's nice to have an action to seal the understanding communicated by the word.

So God also made a way for reassurance. We ought to know that God's word is good. He cannot lie. But the weakness — the frailty — of human faith welcomes an act of reassurance.

A Permanent Sign

The circumstances that first introduced a seal for God's covenant promise also reveal a need. Abraham had witnessed one of the most spectacular divine revelations recorded in human history. God passed between the pieces, committing himself to self-destruction, if necessary, for the fulfillment of the promise of salvation for man (Gen. 15). What more dramatic representation of the commitment of the Lord could be imagined?

Yet in the very next chapter of Genesis Abraham resorts to Hagar his handmaid in an attempt to bring about the fulfillment of the divine promise. Rather than waiting for God to fulfill his own word, Abraham presumes to fix things up by himself. This lapse in the faith of the patriarch

51

shows the need for a more-permanent sign. A vision lasts only for the night and then fades away. Something that will make an abiding mark was needed.

In Genesis 17 God institutes a seal for the promise. He begins by reviewing all that he will do for Abraham in accordance with the covenant (vss 6-8):

> he will make firm his everlasting covenant;
>
> he will include Abraham's descendants in the covenant;
>
> he will be God for Abraham and his seed;
>
> he will give the land to Abraham and his offspring.

All of these things God will do for the patriarch. But what will Abraham do? The Lord is quite pointed: "As for you . . . " (vs 9). The Lord points his finger at Abraham since he will have certain areas of responsibility as well.

"You must keep my covenant." Along with the assurances of the covenant comes an unequivocal injunction. The seal now being established by God must be applied. Every male in Israel will be circumcised at eight days of age. Often it is suggested that the inclusion of infants in the covenant leads to presumption, but the original word of God establishing the seal of this covenant clearly points in the direction of personal responsibility.

Covenant-keeping is an essential part of the covenant's structure. Abraham and his seed (vs 9) must keep the covenant. Far from fostering presumption, the application of the seal of the covenant to children binds them to faithfulness in keeping the vows by which they are obligated in the covenant. If a child sealed in the covenant fails to respond in obedience he cannot presume that he will receive the blessings of the covenant.

Don't be superstitious. Don't think the seal of God's covenant itself has the power to save. Grandparents have been known to sneak into a hospital against the parents' wishes to have an infant with a life-threatening illness baptized. They were superstitious, thinking that baptism itself had the power to save. Beware of such hollow superstition.

Every male at eight days of age was to be circumcised. The responsibility of faithfulness to God's covenant must not be overlooked. "This is my covenant," says the Lord with reference to circumcision (vs 10). The closest possible identification is established between the seal and the covenant. The two are so closely related that it may be said that the seal is the covenant and the covenant is the seal. "Circumcision . . . will be the sign of the covenant" (vs 11). The word used for "sign" includes the idea of both *signifying* and *sealing* a commitment. As a sign, circumcision offered a signal to the world. The hygienic cleansing of circumcision signified the cleansing necessary for consecration to God.

A Permanent Seal

But did circumcision also seal a person in the reality of the cleansing being symbolized? Was circumcision always effective in confirming that a person was in possession of the cleansing that it represented? These questions must be answered from two perspectives.

1. Circumcision was always effective in providing a message to the world. It always signified the need for cleansing from sin and the availability of that cleansing. At the same time it also effectively introduced a person to membership in the externally constituted community of the covenant. These aspects of the ritual of circumcision must not be minimized. By circumcision a testimony was given to the world, and a person was sealed in his membership with the organized community of the covenant.

2. In addition, the sign of the covenant had special significance for those chosen by God for the possession of eternal life according to the mystery of his own will. Circumcision was effective in sealing them in consecration to God as ministered by the Spirit. Whether or not this person had been born again of the Spirit of God at the time of his circumcision, he was by circumcision sealed in the sure possession of the *promise* of God. The one who had been designated by God for eternal salvation before the foundation of the world was sealed by circumcision in the certainty of the ultimate possession of the promises.

These same principles apply to baptism in the new covenant. The ceremony always seals a person into the membership of the organized community of the covenant, the church. But for the elect of God it also seals them in the ultimate possession of the realities associated with consecration to God, including cleansing and forgiveness of sins.

"Every male among you who is eight days old must be circumcised," says the Scripture as it specifies the recipient of the seal of the covenant (vs 12). Contrary to the general practice of Abraham's day, circumcision in this covenant was not a sign of entrance into manhood. Instead it was the formal sign of membership in the covenant community.

"Whether born in your household or bought with your money, they must be circumcised" (vs 13). From the beginning, from the first day of its formation as a covenant community, Israel's membership was wide open to the Gentiles. From the beginning Israel knew nothing of racial purity. Circumcision was not a badge reserved for people of a certain ethnic descent: it was available to men of all nations. This fact continues to have a significant role in any effort to identify the Israel of God, even in the present circumstance. From the beginning God's people Israel could have included in its membership peoples from any of the nations of the world.

"Any uncircumcised male . . . will be cut off from his people" (vs 14). The curse of being cut off from God's people is not descriptive of the circumcised, as though the ceremony sealed a person for curse rather than blessing. Instead the curse is spoken over anyone in the community of the covenant who would neglect the command concerning circumcision. At the same time, a double curse hovers over those who receive the outward sign of cleansing while still continuing without repentance for their sin. Because of special privilege, a special accountability before God must be involved. Whether circumcised as infants or adults, the responsibility associated with circumcision was clear before the Lord. Even as their flesh has received the sign of purification, so their spirit must display purity.

Families and Faith

These verses from Genesis 17 that establish the seal of God's covenant provide many insights into the nature of

God's dealings with humans. A fuller understanding of the biblical faith may be grasped by considering several truths.

1. Physical descent is not enough to make true children of God. To be sealed in a redemptive covenant relation with God a person must undergo a ceremony of cleansing. Circumcision should have been a source of humility for the descendants of Abraham since it testified to the necessity of cleansing from the defilement of sin. Too easily it slipped into being regarded as an indicator that the people of Israel somehow were better than others.

The same principle holds for baptism today. The experience of baptism should bring a person to the point of confessing his sin, his unworthiness, his need for cleansing before God. When the baptized person thinks of himself as better than others he has twisted the basic meaning of the ritual.

2. God deals with families in the bonds of the covenant. The created order of families is not ignored in God's redemptive provisions. God has committed himself to the restoration of family units in his plan of redemption.

It certainly is not proper to trust in natural descent as a basis for hope of redemption. Yet God in his work of redemption does not set nature against grace, the family order of descent over against the spiritual order. It is clear that no one should trust in any supposed merit that he may attach to physical descent as guaranteeing acceptance with God. Yet a believer in Christ should trust in the promises of God concerning the redemption of descendants.

3. Circumcision symbolized inclusion in the community of the covenant. It was not merely a sign of national identity. Instead it related to the heart of the covenant: "I will . . . be your God and the God of your descendants" (Gen. 17:7).

Both circumcision and baptism have been given by God as signs and seals of the covenant of grace. In their application they connect individuals and families with the privileges and responsibilities of being in covenant with God. As signs and seals they are intended to provide a source of assurance for God's people that they belong to the Lord. When coupled with faith they confirm a person in the possession of the blessings of the covenant.

Review Questions

1. What are some of the ways that people seal a promise?
2. What is distinctive about the seal that God gives Abraham in Genesis 17?
3. What parallels can you see between the New Testament sign and seal that has replaced the seal given to Abraham?

Discussion Questions

1. How has baptism helped your faith and your ability to be a parent (if you are one)?
2. What would you say to parents of a baptized child who is eighteen and does not yet believe the gospel?

7

HOPE FOR YOUR HOUSE

There can be no question but that the children of those who professed faith in the God of Abraham received the seal of the covenant. The command was given specifically to Abraham: at eight days of age the child was to receive the sign and seal of circumcision. That command was in effect for 2000 years from the days of Abraham to the days of Jesus Christ.

What did circumcision mean to the children of the old covenant? It meant the same thing it meant for adults. Whether infants or adults, circumcision sealed them into membership with the externally constituted people of God. At the same time, if the person receiving circumcision was the elect of God it also sealed him in the possession, sooner or later, of the spiritual promises of the covenant. The cutting away of the foreskin by circumcision was a symbolic act of cleansing. It represented the removal of the sinful nature. Whether or not he was a regenerate believer at that time, the act of circumcision still sealed the chosen of the Lord in the ultimate possession of spiritual cleansing.

It is also clear that the old-covenant people of God practiced what might be dubbed, in modern parlance, "believer's circumcision." Any Gentile who confessed the God of Israel would receive the sign of circumcision. In this regard it is interesting to note that the old-covenant people of

COVENANTS: GOD'S WAY WITH HIS PEOPLE

God were more stringent in their demands for evidence of the validity of faith than is generally practiced in churches today. The confession that led to circumcision had to be confirmed by life not just once but consistently thereafter.

If a circumcised person committed idolatry he must be put to death, cut off from the people of God. If a circumcised person whispered to his neighbor, "Let's go after other gods," he must be put to death — cut off from the people of God. Far more than is the normal practice of the church today, God's people under the old covenant were striving to see that only true confessors continued in the covenant. They practiced confessor's circumcision in the best possible sense. Yet they circumcised infants!

Babies Too

Why also infants?

1. Because God commanded it.

2. Because God said the children were in the covenant.

3. Because they perceived it as a way of blessing for themselves *and* their children.

4. Because they were claiming the intent of God to restore families in his work of redemption.

That was the practice of the old covenant. For 2000 years God's people understood his covenant as including their families.

The essence of the covenant by which men and women are saved today is the same as it was then. The covenant that binds sinners to a holy God is founded on the blood of the everlasting covenant shed by Christ before the foundation of the world. His was the actual sacrifice that made acceptable the offerings of the old-covenant people.

The signs and seals of old and new covenants are also the same in essence. As Colossians 2:11, 12 says:

> In him you were also circumcised, in the putting off of the sinful nature, not with a circumcision done by the hands of men but with the circumcision done by Christ, having been buried with him in baptism.

By being buried with Christ in baptism, you were circumcised. So reads the word of God. It is difficult to imagine a mode of expression that would establish a closer connection between two religious ceremonies than the connection indicated in these verses. Old-covenant circumcision was in essence the equivalent of new-covenant baptism. In this context you can find hope for your house. As the children of believers were included in the fellowship of the old covenant, so they are included today.

New Covenant Households

This hope is reinforced by a look at the actual practice of applying the new-covenant seal of baptism. Ten New Testament passages speak of actual baptisms under various circumstances. The pattern established in these baptisms provides hope for your house, for they indicate that you can claim by faith that your children belong to God through the covenant.

1. Acts 2:38, 39: "Repent and be baptized, every one of you . . . . The promise is for you and your children and for all who are far off — for all whom the Lord our God will call." How would the people hearing Peter's sermon on the Day of Pentecost have understood this statement about their children? The question may be answered partially by considering the kind of nursery facilities that were available on the Day of Pentecost.

There *were* no nursery facilities. Children were considered as a vital part of the worshiping community (cf Deut. 29:11; Josh. 24:15). For 2000 years children had been *in* the covenant, having received the sign of the covenant. Are the children to be put out of the covenant now? Having begun the Day of Pentecost with their children included in God's covenant promises, are they who believed Peter's sermon to end the day with their children outside the promises of the covenant? Peter's assurance that the promise was "for you and your children" declares the opposite. With their believing parents they are in the covenant.

2. Acts 8:12: "But when they believed . . . they were baptized, both men and women." This answers the question of women in the new covenant. In this case women are specifically indicated as receiving the sign of the covenant. Perhaps you have wondered about the place of women in the old covenant. Were they left out because they did not receive the sign of circumcision? No, they were not left out. By the circumcision of a woman's father or husband she was included in the covenant.

Does the fact that women are specified as receiving the sign of the new covenant indicate that the family bond no longer operates with respect to the sign of the new covenant? No — the new place of women as recipients of the covenantal seal is quite appropriate in view of the fact that the eternal state is closer now than it was under the old covenant. In eternity men and women will neither marry nor be given in marriage. This nearness of the eternal state of the world finds one symbolic representation by the inclusion of women in the covenant as distinctive persons.

But nothing in this text indicates that God was not also continuing to work in family units under the provisions of the new covenant. So long as marriage and family continue, the promises of the covenant also continue. The enrichment of the symbolism of the new covenant does not imply a loss of any of the blessings of the old.

3. Acts 8:38: "Then both Philip and the eunuch went down into the water, and Philip baptized him." By the baptism of the Ethiopian eunuch the question about the inclusion of a single man in the new covenant is answered. Can this stranger be included in the covenant too? Yes! Apart from previous family bonds, a complete stranger can be joined to the covenant family of God.

4. Acts 9:18: "Immediately, something like scales fell from Saul's eyes, and he could see again. He got up and was baptized." What about an enemy of the gospel? Can a persecutor of the faith be brought into the fellowship of the covenant? Indeed he can! The greatest enemy of God's people can be transformed, baptized and commissioned as the greatest missionary of all time.

5. Acts 10:2, 44, 48: "[Cornelius] and all his family were devout and God-fearing . . . [T]he Holy Spirit came on all who heard the message. . . . So he ordered that they be

baptized in the name of Jesus Christ." Clearly now a household situation is involved. All the house of Cornelius are said to be devout and to believe in the gospel. At the point of baptism, the household is not explicitly mentioned, but the implication is clear. A gentile household, including rambunctious teenage children (assuming some may have been present) are sealed in the possession of the promise of the new covenant. As in Israel of old, the covenant is made with all the house.

6. Acts 16:14, 15: "The Lord opened [Lydia's] heart to respond to Paul's message. When she and the members of her household were baptized, she invited us to her home." Now the situation is still different: a woman is being baptized. In this case she appears to be serving as head of her house and no mention is made of her husband. More specifically, the Scripture says that she believed and that she and her house were baptized. Did her children believe? The Scripture doesn't say.

The important thing to note is that the baptism was by household. Lydia functioned as the representative head of her family. Without resorting to an argument from silence, it may be asserted that the pattern being formed for new-covenant baptisms is one of household baptisms, whatever that means. In this case only Lydia is said to believe, but her whole house is baptized.

7. Acts 16:31-34: A literal translation of verse 31 reads as follows: "You [singular] believe . . . and you [singular] will be saved, you [singular] and your house." The verse sounds very much like Peter's words at Pentecost. But here the word *house* rather than *children* is used, suggesting

a more specific allusion to the old-covenant inclusion of the house in the application of the seal of the covenant.

"Then they spoke the word of the Lord to him *with* all in his house" (vs 32). The NIV states that Paul spoke to him *and* to all the others in his house. A more literal reading of the better text states that Paul spoke to him *with* all his house. The difference is slight but of some significance. Was a baby in the jailer's arms? The passage doesn't say. But once more it is the house with which Paul and Silas are dealing.

"And immediately he and all his house were baptized . . . and he rejoiced wholehousedly, he having believed in God" (vss 33, 34). The word translated "wholehousedly" is an adverb, which may modify either a verb or another adverb. But it is rather strange to treat an adverb as though it were the subject of a verb. The NIV translation makes this single adverb to serve as the subject of two separate verbs: "The *whole family* was filled with joy, because *they* had come to believe" (emphasis added). But actually the parts of the sentence are: singular verb ("he rejoiced"), modifying adverb ("wholehousedly") and singular modifying participle ("he having believed").

Did the newly converted jailer toss a toddler upward as a joyous expression of his new-found faith? Is that what is meant by rejoicing wholehousedly? The text is not explicit. But it is clear again that household baptism was the practice of the apostles with respect to the Philippian jailer.

8. Acts 18:8: "Crispus . . . and his entire household believed in the Lord; and many of the Corinthians who heard him believed and were baptized." In this case it is

specifically stated that all the house of Crispus believed along with him. Mature children believe, and they all are baptized. That fact in itself is a wonder of God's grace and should not be ignored. The whole family is joyously united in faith.

9. Acts 19:5-7: "On hearing this, they were baptized into the name of the Lord Jesus. . . . [T]hey spoke in tongues . . . . There were about twelve men in all." At the predominantly gentile city of Ephesus a mini-Pentecost occurs. Upon baptism twelve men (like the original twelve apostles in Acts 2) spoke in foreign tongues. Following the pattern of "Jerusalem, Judea, Samaria and the uttermost part of the earth," the outpouring of the Spirit at Ephesus represents the outer circumference of the expanding coverage of the world by the gospel. This outpouring of the Spirit on twelve men seems intentionally to echo the events of Pentecost and to mark the prosperity of the gospel in the gentile world.

10. 1 Corinthians 1:14, 16: "I did not baptize any of you except Crispus and Gaius . . . [and] the household of Stephanas." Once more reference is made to household baptism. While individuals are designated as the recipients of baptism, a whole household also is included.

In considering the occurrences of baptism in the new covenant, a marvelous diversity appears. First a large crowd of Jewish people are baptized. Then women specifically are said to be included. Then a single man. Then a gentile family. Then a woman as the head of her house along with her family. Then a whole family of believers. Then the twelve men of Ephesus. Just about every kind of case imaginable is depicted. Jew and Gentile, young and old, single and married, men and women.

Yet one pattern that emerges with great regularity clearly should give "hope to your house." Of the ten instances recorded, six refer explicitly to children or to households: Pentecost, Cornelius, Lydia, the Philippian jailer, Crispus and Stephanas. Of the remaining four instances, two concern bachelors who *had* no house (Paul and the Ethiopian eunuch). The case of the twelve Ephesian men appears to be a special circumstance emphasizing the repetition of the principles of Pentecost.

So in six out of seven cases in the new covenant where the baptism of a household might have been anticipated, the fact of household baptism is explicitly mentioned! The point is plain: God is concerned to redeem families, not merely individuals. To show his concern he includes family units in his covenant. Indeed, it is not explicitly stated that infants were present in any one of the households mentioned; but the clear fact of new-covenant baptismal practice is that it was according to households.

Hope for Today's Homes

The explicit practice of the 2000 years of the same covenant of redemption from Abraham to Christ provides the historical foundation for this new-covenant practice of household baptism. The families of Abraham, Moses and David are provided with the same way of redemption through the blood of Christ; and each of these successive covenants mentions explicitly the inclusion of children. The prophecy of Jeremiah concerning the new covenant also speaks of God's continuing commitment to redeem households (Jer. 31:31, 33).

There is hope for your house. The promises are for you and your house. By bringing yourself and your children for baptism, you claim by faith the promises of God's covenant. As you and your children respond in faith to God's grace you will see the full manifestation of his grace in redeeming a people to himself.

Review Questions

1. Where does the book of Acts refer to household baptisms?

2. What hope is offered for your home by the biblical teaching on baptism?

Discussion Questions

1. Describe how you imagine the families in Acts 2:38, 39; 10:2, 44, 48; 16:14, 15; 16:31-34; 18:8; 1 Corinthians 1:14, 16 worshiped together and talked over spiritual things. Think about their background, spiritual history, distinctive makeup, etc.

2. What new ideas about how your family ought to relate to Christ are suggested by what you have learned from this chapter?

8

PRECEPTS AND PROBLEMS

Moses: The Covenant of Law (I)

Law creates problems. To introduce the category of law into covenant invariably stirs up controversy. It's one thing to talk about the beauties of oneness with God, of fellowship with the Creator, of harmony in the covenant; it's another thing to talk about rules, requirements, duties or commands. The very mention of these strictures smashes the sense of comfortable communion with the Maker.

Law speaks of standardization, of conformity to an outward norm. In the minds of many it implies coercion. But *covenant* suggests relationship, trust and friendship. The very idea of a covenant of law seems incongruous. Yet here it is — the covenant of law.

The role of law in the life of man has always created controversy. In the present as well as in previous generations law has meant trouble. Among equally devoted, well-meaning, gifted people the subject of law often creates more heat than light. Yet it's unquestionably true that the single covenant in the Bible receiving the fullest elaboration is the Mosaic covenant of law. The subject simply cannot be avoided, which must mean God doesn't want his people to avoid this subject.

By way of introduction, remember that the idea of covenant is larger than the concept of law. Covenant may embrace all aspects of law; but law as a category cannot exhaust all the various elements of covenant.

Law may be perceived both as a portrait and a mirror. As a portrait, law outlines the features of the image of God to which man is to be conformed. Law draws a picture of the Creator so that man can see clearly the shape of the One with whom he is to have fellowship. Only as conformity to that shape is achieved will fellowship be possible.

At the same time, law serves as a mirror. Law enables us to see ourselves as we really are and to compare our image with the shape to which we ought to conform. If disfigurations or misshapen aspects of personhood are present, the mirror of the law will make those points painfully obvious to us.

An inherent problem associated with the revelation of law in covenant is the achieving of a balance between standardization and individuality. Law provides a basic framework for the man or woman who intends to conform to the image of God. But because of the uniqueness of each individual and his or her own peculiar relation to the Creator, law in its universal categories cannot define all the details of each person's obligation to the Creator.

One of the greatest problems for people in covenant with God is finding the balance between enforcement of law-principles and acknowledgment of individual liberties. This matter of balance is complicated by the progressive unfolding of the legal expectations of the God of the covenant. In the processes of the revelation of law in Scripture, the permanently abiding principles of God's will are encased in temporary legislation that must pass away at a later stage. Distinguishing between the abiding kernel and the temporally conditioned husk of God's law supplies the supreme challenge to a person wanting to understand God's will.

The Law Is Special

It is tempting to set Mosaic law over against Abrahamic promise. One popular viewpoint suggests that Israel should not so rashly have accepted the provisions of the Mosaic covenant of law at Mount Sinai. Instead the nation should have pleaded humbly for a longer period under the gracious provisions of the Abrahamic covenant of promise.

In this same connection it is easy to read some of the assertions of the apostle Paul as though they intended to present the covenant of Moses as being diametrically opposed to the covenant of Abraham, for he explicitly states, "The law is not based on faith" (Gal. 3:12). If context is not considered, this statement appears to proclaim that law has nothing to do with the promise received by faith.

A common scheme for the three successive covenants in the Old Testament is as follows:

Abraham — an unconditional covenant of promise;
Moses — a conditional covenant of law;
David — an unconditional covenant of promise.

This popular perspective on the Mosaic covenant of law requires careful attention. At stake is the larger question of the relation of the new-covenant believer today to each of these older covenants.

Some effort must be made to capture the essence of the Mosaic covenant for what it is in itself. After all, despite all the objections to law, the Mosaic covenant represents a major phase in the redemptive revelation of God to man in his sin. Specifically, the distinguishing characteristic of the Mosaic covenant may be defined as "an external summation of the will of God." Its unique contribution to the progress of revelation is that it summarizes in brief form the holy will of God for men.

The Mosaic record of Sinai itself supports this analysis. Reference is made to the "ten words" (the Ten Commandments) as the words of the covenant (cf Ex. 34:28; Deut. 4:13). Although a revelation far more extensive than the Ten Commandments was communicated at Sinai, the ten words can be equated with the covenant itself.

The distinctiveness of this new stage in the progress of God's revelation must be recognized. Never before had God explicitly laid out in such a clear summary the pattern of life to which he expected men to conform. These laws had always been present as eternal truths, but they had never been laid out in such a clear fashion. Because these Ten Commandments arise out of the nature of God himself, they were anything but arbitrarily constructed dicta that were suddenly introduced for the first time at Sinai.

God has always been spirit and therefore could only be insulted by the erection of an idol. So he commanded: "No graven images." From creation he had sanctified the Sabbath day, calling on man to reflect his own pattern of work and rest. So he commanded: "Rest on the seventh day."

Each one of the Ten Commandments finds its origin in the nature of God, but only at Sinai were they summarized in such a perfected form. Although these moral laws of God were inherent in the image of God in man from the time of man's creation, the corruptions of sin had the effect of blurring the clarity of these laws. At Sinai the will of God for man made in God's image once more becomes clear.

Once this event of revelation had occurred the world could never be the same. All to whom this law is proclaimed suddenly bear the responsibility of a full accountability to their Maker and can never again claim innocence before the law. Men may be driven to despair by the law but they may not claim guiltlessness.

In considering the convicting character of the revelation of God's law in the Mosaic covenant a basic confusion must be avoided. The Mosaic covenant of law must not be confused with the original covenant of works made with Adam, the original man, while he was still in his innocence. In the original circumstance the innocent, sinless man was offered no provisions for blessing in the event of disobedience. If Adam broke God's law he died: no promised way of relief was ever hinted at. But the historical circumstance of the Mosaic covenant was entirely different. God had already redeemed Israel from the judgment of death for their sin by the blood of the Passover lamb. They already had experienced the blessing of God despite their sin.

With the law code there was the provision of sacrifice in the event of sin. Under the Mosaic covenant, transgression of the law was presumed and provision for forgiveness was graciously provided. It is a legalistic twisting of the intent and content of the Mosaic covenant that transforms this gracious ordering into a covenant of works. The covenant of law under Moses and the promise of redemption under Abraham go hand in hand because *both* manifest God's gracious will to redeem.

The law that came under Moses neither disannulled nor interrupted the promise given Abraham. Both worked together as a basic unity. Both served the same end of bringing fallen man to redemption. The basic distinctives of the Mosaic covenant of law agree with the Abrahamic covenant of promise. Both covenants combine to fill out the picture of a gracious God's plan to redeem sinful men.

We Still Need the Law

What about the place of the Mosaic covenant today? Doesn't the Bible teach that we are not under law but under grace (Rom. 6:14)? Indeed it does! But what do the words mean? Certainly "you are not under law" doesn't mean that you can steal, kill, lie, scorn your parents and blaspheme God all you like, does it? Of course not!

Most likely Paul is referring to your personal law-keeping as it relates to your being found legally just before God. You don't have to keep God's law perfectly for yourself to be declared guiltless. If that were the case, who would have a hope?

The law had to be kept—and Jesus Christ kept the law *for* you and for all who would trust his grace for salvation. But you are not under the obligation to keep God's law for yourself in order to be found legally just before God.

At the same time, the law of God continues to have significance for your daily life. Consider three ways in which it is obvious that you must live in accordance with the law of God *just because* you are a forgiven Christian:

1. The fullest state of blessing in the life of the Christian comes from keeping the law of God. This point is illustrated specifically with respect to the fifth commandment. According to Paul, Christian children should obey their parents for this "is the first commandment with a promise" (Eph. 6:2). Long life on the earth is promised by God to those who honor their parents. This blessing is reserved for the obedient.

Jesus explicitly declared that he had not come to destroy the law or the prophets but to fulfill their requirements. He further stated that anyone who breaks one of the least of the commandments of the law would be called least in the kingdom of God (Matt. 5:17-19). He insisted that the wise man must build his life on the firm foundation of keeping God's commandments. Only this kind of life would experience the blessing of stability (Matt. 7:24-27).

It's a privilege to know God's law as it has been revealed in the Ten Commandments. Your life will experience the fullest blessing as you keep God's law.

2. Chastening will come to those who violate God's law. It's obvious that Israel got into trouble every time they neglected the law of God. Whenever they lusted in the wilderness they suffered chastening from the hand of the Lord. When they erected idols like the other nations they were carried away into captivity.

The same principle works among the Christians of the new covenant. "[T]he Lord disciplines those he loves" (Heb. 12:6) refers to an experience common to old-covenant as well as new-covenant saints. In the experience of the Corinthian Christians, severe chastening from the hand of the Lord came when some of their number abused the holiness of God by their behavior at the Lord's table (1 Cor. 11:30-32).

These warnings to all violators of God's law continue until today. No one can ignore God's law with impunity. Even people living under the gracious provisions of the new covenant must remember this principle.

3. Christians under the new covenant will be evaluated on the day of judgment by the deeds they have done, whether good or evil (2 Cor. 5:10). A consistent picture emerges in Scripture: salvation is by faith but judgment is by works. Indeed men will enter that awesome judgment scene either as sheep on the right hand or as goats on the left (Matt. 25:31-33); but the judgment will be in accord with the deeds done in the body, whether good or evil. This basis for judgment applies to people living today as well as in Moses's day.

It would be well for Christians who have been saved by the sacrificial death of Christ to give fuller consideration to this principle. Christ not only *died for you*: he *lives in you*. By faith you may claim his transforming power for your life. You may receive strength from the living Christ to walk according to his will.

The Mosaic covenant of law may be seen as relating organically to the whole of redemptive history. Down to the present era the law of God continues to play a role of paramount importance. Rather than becoming a relic of the past it continues to have significance until the consummation.

Review Questions

1. How is the law a portrait? How is it a mirror?

2. Choose any two of the ten commandments. What does the first show you about God? What does the other teach you about yourself?

3. What is distinctive about the Mosaic covenant?

Discussion Questions

1. If you are "not under the law but under grace," why should you live according to the law of God?

2. Choose one of the ten commandments that governs an area of your life that needs improvement. Use the following questions to develop a plan of obedience: (a) How does this portrait of God suggest what I should be like? (b) What is the first step I should take to become like this? (c) When can I take that step? (d) Who will help me? how? (e) What encouragements are implied by the commandments that I can claim?

9

PROGRESS BY PRECEPTS

Moses: The Covenant of Law (II)

Something there is that doesn't love a wall,
That sends the frozen ground-swell under it,
And spills the upper boulders in the sun . . .

My apple trees will never get across
And eat the cones under his pines, I tell him. . . .

Something there is that doesn't love a wall.

— Robert Frost, *Mending Walls* (1913)

Something there is that doesn't love a law. Something there is in mankind that will do everything it can to circumvent a law, to ignore a law, to resist a law. Yet law is a blessing from God.

What would life be like if there were no law of gravity? Why, you couldn't even drink a glass of water. If there were no moral law against stealing you could never leave your grocery cart outside the store while you went to get your car. All your carefully picked groceries would be gone before you returned.

Law as an Improvement

To appreciate the ever-increasing value of the revelation of law in Scripture it is necessary to understand how much better the circumstances were for God's people under Moses than for all the previous ages. As a seed grows to a sapling and matures into a fruit-bearing tree, so the revelation of God's law progressed throughout the history of redemption. The entirety of the will of God was implicit from the beginning just as the seed contains all. But the progressive unfolding of the specifics of God's law displays an advancement that moves toward the fullest revelation in the new covenant.

For some interpreters of the Bible the revelation of the law at Sinai meant a serious step of retrogression for Israel. As indicated in the previous chapter, some have proposed that, instead of rashly accepting the condition of the Mosaic covenant of law, Israel should have pleaded humbly for an extension of time under the gracious provisions of the Abrahamic covenant of promise.

Such a perspective hardly does justice to the scene at Sinai. God himself appears at the top of the mountain. Smoke, fire, earthquake and an ever-louder trumpet blast accompany the coming of the Lord. He delivers the legal summation of his will in an authoritative fashion that could be characteristic only of God. "Everything the LORD has said we will do" is the only appropriate response to the dictates of this divine law (cf Ex. 24:3).

It must not be forgotten that provision for forgiveness was integral to the revelation of the law at Sinai. The Lord was not demanding a commitment that was impossible for his redeemed people. He made ample provision for relief from condemnation through the sacrificial system. Also the demands of the Mosaic covenant of law were in essence no different from the devotion to God required of

Abraham. Under the covenant of promise the patriach was required to walk before the Lord with the total commitment of his life (Gen. 17:1). This commitment involved the same obedience to God's will that is required of every Christian as he confesses the lordship of Christ in his life.

Better Four Ways

In what sense was an *advancement* made in the Mosaic covenant? Four areas in particular may be noted.

First, the Mosaic covenant of law formed Israel into a *national entity*. The Abrahamic covenant functioned well for a nomadic people in the days of the patriarchs, but the complexities of national life required a more ordered society. The Mosaic covenant provided that needed order.

Second, the Mosaic covenant exceeded the previous epochs in terms of the *comprehensiveness* of the revelation of God's will for his people. With a fuller understanding of the law of God, Israel possessed a better knowledge of the God of the covenant himself. Also, a comprehensive revelation of God's will acts as a deterrent against faulty expectations about a person's walk with God. Some erroneous views about the possibility of perfection in this life suggest that man can be free from all known sin. No more dangerous position could be imagined! If a person has been exposed to a comprehensive representation of God's will he is far less likely to slip into such inadequate self-evaluations.

Third, the Mosaic covenant of law represents an advancement in that this revelation of law has a greater capacity to *humble* men and women. The more they are made aware of their sin the more ready they will be to flee to Christ.

Fourth, the Mosaic covenant of law provided a fuller picture of the *holiness* expected of the people of God. His people were to be a royal priesthood, reflecting the glories of a holy God.

So the full statement of God's law in Moses's day must not be received as a backward step in the processes of redemption. Instead this law means fuller life for the redeemed. At the same time, the Mosaic covenant was far less in its glory than what followed in the orderly unfolding of God's will for his people. Particularly when compared with the brilliant light of the new covenant, the revelation of the Mosaic covenant of law is seen to be inferior.

The Law Today

In laying out the drastic difference between the lettered form of the Mosaic covenant and the Spirit-filled, life-giving form of the new covenant, Paul comments on the human tendency to cling to the old shadows despite the greater glories of the new reality. Considering the externalized form of the old, it may be characterized as a ministry of death and condemnation (2 Cor. 3:7-9). The God of the covenant certainly was present to give life through the Mosaic covenant; yet its form was one of externalized shadows that had not the power to give life.

"Even to this day" a veil covers the face of men and women when they read the law of Moses, says Paul (2 Cor. 3:15). The temporal, temporary, limited character of the Mosaic covenant is hidden from their eyes. When compared to all other forms of religion the law appears in such glory that it cannot be perceived as temporally conditioned and fading in its glory. The Jewish community of today reads the Old Testament law with this veil over their eyes. They compare the Mosaic code with all other religious systems, and are so convinced of its superior quality that they cannot think of a more glorious form of religion.

But whenever they turn to the Lord that veil will be removed (2 Cor. 3:16). How could the Mosaic sacrifices for sin ever compare in value to the sacrifice of the Son of God? What is the display of God's glory in the tabernacle in the wilderness when compared to the effulgence of God's glory radiating from the Son?

Some who claim Christ wish to cling to dietary and ceremonial laws of the Mosaic covenant, not recognizing that these things are done away in Christ. For awhile these laws were important as a model for teaching holiness. Like scaffolding on a skyscraper or the shell encasing a nut, these ceremonial laws served a temporary purpose until the final product had been formed.

One brief comment of the Son of God incarnate (cf Mark 7:15, 19) has the legal power to eliminate stipulations of the Mosaic covenant that had been in force for centuries. "Nothing [i.e., no food] outside a man can make him 'unclean' by going into him. . . . (In saying this, Jesus declared all foods 'clean.')" Some may be so impressed with the majesty of Mosaic legislation that they cannot conceive of its repeal, but Jesus' words are unmistakable. All foods are to be received with thanksgiving, giving glory to God the Redeemer.

Current attitudes toward the seventh-day Sabbath also fail to appreciate the newness of the new covenant. It is true that the essential principle of one day's rest in seven remains inviolable: the fourth commandment remains embedded in the permanent frame of the ten words. But must the seventh day rather than the first continue to be sanctified as the time for rest and worship?

According to John 20:19, 26 the Lord rose from the dead and set a pattern of appearing to his disciples on the first day of the week. According to Acts 20:7 the breaking of bread and the preaching of the word occurred on the first day of the week. According to 1 Corinthians 16:2 the regular offerings of the church were made on the first day of the week. According to Revelation 1:10 the apostle John was in the Spirit on the Lord's Day, which indicates that Christ's resurrection had the effect of claiming one day of the week as peculiarly his own. By showing his power over death on this day he communicated to his disciples that this day was peculiarly his own. While the old-covenant law looked forward to a coming day of rest by the symbol of the seventh day, the new-covenant life celebrates a rest of redemption that has now been won.

What about Theonomy?

The advancement of the new covenant beyond the old is partially denied also by those who have a high respect for the civil laws of Israel. Called "Theonomists," these people are impressed with the equity and wisdom of the laws that governed the state of Israel — and rightly so. Particularly when compared with the laws as enforced by the secular state today, the civic order of the state of Israel under the old covenant magnifies the glories of a holy God.

Yet the limited value of the old-covenant state of Israel as a typological model of the kingdom of God must be recognized. Its domain was spatially defined by the divinely set boundaries of Palestine. Within those boundaries the land was to have a civic division by lot among the physical descendants of the twelve tribes of Israel.

This legislation was never intended to be carried out in the territory of Assyria or Egypt (thinking only of Israel's nearest neighbors). Although calculated to reveal the equity of God in land distribution, this legislation was temporal in its application, limited to the time of Israel's presence as an organized nation in Palestine under the provisions of the old covenant.

In the early colonialization of America some efforts were made to reinstitute the civil codes of Israel. The laws of New England as printed in 1641 were patterned on the tribal territorial rights of ancient Israel; so properties normally had to be sold to others already inhabiting a town (thus keeping the appointed land within the "tribe"). Daughters inheriting land were to marry within the constituency of the town or pay a rent charge to the public treasury of the town. But such efforts to transfer a tribally arranged theocracy into a modern civil community involve a great deal of imaginative stretching. While general principles of equity might transfer, the old-covenant laws of a civic nature could not have the binding effect of the ten words.

Particularly because of the enforcement of the true religion by civic authorities according to Mosaic law, it becomes clear that the legislation of the old covenant envisions a theocratic government that does not fit the intentions of God for the spread of the gospel in the present era. According to Deuteronomy 13:5, the prophet who promotes a false religion must be put to death. According to Deuteronomy 13:6-11, if anyone even of your own household secretly proposes the worship of another god he must be put to death. According to Deuteronomy 13:12-18, if an entire community pursues the worship of a false god the whole community must be destroyed.

Such procedures may be helpful in depicting the thoroughness of the last judgment. They may provide a basis for excommunication from the church of Christ. But to ask the secular state of today — even a Christianized state — to enforce such laws could only bring on society once more the horrors of the religious wars of previous centuries.

By the common grace of God the civil powers of today may perform a limited function in restraining evil among a fallen humanity. For this reason they deserve the honor that properly belongs to state government. But the glories of the old-covenant model must not be confused with the limited functions of the state in the present age. The Lord of the new covenant personally acknowledged the place of the state today in distinction from his own kingdom when he declared, "Give to Caesar what is Caesar's, and to God what is God's" (Matt. 22:21).

One day the true religion will be enforced by the true state. But that day will come only with the return of Christ in glory when he establishes the eternal kingdom of God.

In the meantime the Christian must not be blinded by the glories of the old-covenant revelation, failing to see the greater glory of the grace of the new covenant as it is manifest to men of all nations.

The new-covenant kingdom is superior to the typological model of the old-covenant era. Greater grace is shown to all the nations. Greater concentration is placed on the permanently abiding moral law of God. Greater glory is found in the person of Christ the anointed King, who has poured out his Spirit on all flesh.

COVENANTS: GOD'S WAY WITH HIS PEOPLE

Review Questions

1. List the ways that the Mosaic covenant is an advance over the Abrahamic covenant.

2. List your impressions and reactions to the role of the Mosaic law in current Judaism, in Seventh-Day Adventism, in dispensationalism and in theonomy. What questions do you have about the role of the Mosaic law today?

Discussion Questions

1. Outline how you would use the material in this lesson in a conversation with a Jewish person. If you have a Jewish coworker or friend, tailor your outline to that person's ideas and needs.

2. In what sense should the modern state legislate morality according to Mosaic law? In what sense should they not?

10

THE KING IS COMING

David: The Covenant of the Kingdom

Now the kingdom comes! The climax of the old covenant is found in the coming of the kingdom in David's day. The seed of the woman destined to crush the head of the serpent is revealed to be a kingly seed. The preservation of the earth from violence, as promised to Noah, will be maintained by a single sovereign who will restrain the wicked through terrifying the lawbreaker. The land promised to Abraham, having the same dimensions as the territory of the Davidic monarchy, will be governed by a righteous adminstration. The law's greatest blessing will be showered on God's people through the charitable rule of the lawgiver who sits enthroned on Mount Zion.

The Throne Secured

This coming centers on the security of the king's throne. When the king sits on his throne the kingdom has come. That principle is true both for the old-covenant and the new-covenant eras. For this reason it is most important to be aware of the precise historical circumstance in which the king's throne is secured.

The establishment of the covenant of the kingdom is recorded in 2 Samuel 7. In this chapter God confirms his covenant promise to King David. Three events set the stage.

1. David conquered Jerusalem (2 Sam. 5). This event symbolized a step toward unifying God's people in a stronger bond under a single leader. Until the capture of Jerusalem David had ruled from Hebron, deep in the interior of the southern tribes. This arrangement had developed naturally since David was a descendant of Judah, whose tribal allotment was in the southernmost portion of Palestine.

Jerusalem was a no-man's-land straddling the center of the two major segments of Israel's populace. It still remained in the hands of the Jebusites. By taking Jerusalem and locating his throne in that place David took a giant step toward unifying the nation. Even as the District of Columbia was carved out of states north and south to provide a neutral locale for the new capital of the United States, so Jerusalem's situation naturally made it a place where the nation of Israel could unify around its king.

2. David brought the ark to Jerusalem (2 Sam. 6). The ark of the covenant represented the throne of God. It was the place from which God exercised his lordship on earth. The Holy One dwelt between the cherubim and dispensed his power among the nations of the world from that point.

This action represented the merger of the human throne of the Davidic kingship with the throne of God. David's greatest desire was that his rule as king would be nothing more and nothing less than a manifestation of God's rule on earth.

Before David brought the ark to his royal city of Jerusalem the earthly representation of the throne of God might have been in one place and the throne of Israel's king in another. David sought a harmonization of his lordship with the Lord's own rule. He desired to bring his domain under the direct authority of God. This action of bringing the ark of God to Jerusalem was a most important forerunner to the establishment of the Davidic covenant.

3. David finally found rest from all his enemies (2 Sam. 7:1). That's what the kingdom of God is all about. The king of Israel rules in security, with all his enemies brought under his feet because he rules on behalf of the eternal God.

From these circumstances surrounding the security of David's throne by divine covenant some insight can be gained into the present rule of Jesus Christ, the King of the new covenant. His coronation occurred at his resurrection and ascension to the right hand of the Father shortly after his humiliation and burial.

By his resurrection and ascension Christ "ascended on high" and "led captives in his train" (Eph. 4:7-13). By ascending to the heavenly Jerusalem, the Mount Zion from which God reigns, Jesus Christ merged God's domain with his own messianic throne. All power in heaven and earth now belongs to him even as it does to God. Having been seated at the right hand of God's power he exercises sovereignty over people and nations on behalf of God the Father. All of these aspects of Christ's lordship were anticipated in shadow form by the establishment of the Davidic throne.

The setting of the establishment of David's throne under the old covenant helps us understand the present rule of Christ. By his ascension to the right hand of the Father he has merged the messianic throne with the eternal lordship of God.

The Person on the Throne

Apart from the appearance of that individual who is to serve as king, the circumstances leading up to the security of the kingdom have no meaning. The kingdom cannot come without the king. Thus the key verse of the Davidic covenant is 2 Samuel 7:14. In this verse God tells David that his descendant who rules after him will be designated as God's own son: "I will be his father, and he will be my son."

It may not be startling in a day of overfamiliarity with God to read of a man who will be known as God's son, but from an old-covenant perspective this type designation was almost unthinkable. God was too great for such a relationship of intimacy to be imagined!

Indeed, Israel as a nation was called God's son (Ex. 4:22, 23; Hos. 11:1). But never was an individual person designated as son of God — yet here it is! The descendant of David who rules in God's behalf over God's kingdom receives the designation "son of God."

This principle of a descendant from David who is God's son finds its climactic fulfillment in Jesus the Christ. As the realization of the old-covenant promise it is in the fullest sense God who rules from David's throne (see Heb. 1:5).

Out of this principle of the centrality of the king as God's son arise two major emphases in this covenant.

First, the king serves as covenant mediator. Throughout the history of David's monarchy the king mediated the covenant among God's people. He represented the people before God and God before the people. The king had the power to initiate covenant commitments on behalf of the people and the power to plead for them with God on the basis of the covenant. The king in Israel's structure did not formally fulfill the office of a priest; but as son he had access to the Father, and so fulfilled the role of intercessor *for* the people as well as ruler *over* the people.

Ultimately this role of a king who intercedes also finds its perfection in the person of Jesus Christ. His dual role as priest-king is not according to the order of Levi, who was only a priest. Instead he is a king who is a priest according to the order of Melchizedek, who was "king of righteousness" while at the same time serving as a compassionate priest (cf Heb. 7:1ff).

This concept of the king as covenant mediator affects *your* life. It means that your king is your priest. The one who rules over you is identical with the one who pleads for you. In other words, your advocate is your judge—the one who pleads for you is the same as the one who enforces judgments about you! Your king is your priest and your priest is your king.

Second, the promised Davidic king is God's Son. This priestly King as Son rules over God's people forever. The Son who rules in God's kingdom will continue on his throne throughout eternity. David's house, kingdom and throne are established forever (2 Sam. 7:16).

God's faithfulness to this promise is foreshadowed by the fact that David's line and Jerusalem's throne were maintained under the old covenant for a period of over 400 years. This tenure probably represents the longest single dynasty in the history of the world. It may be contrasted immediately with the experience of the northern kingdom of Israel. Within its 200-year history the northern kingdom had a dozen different families as rulers, with four different capitals.

Yet the nagging question cannot be suppressed: how can we explain the fact that the kingship of the Davidic line eventually was interrupted? Even though the promise concerning the rule of David's son spoke of an eternal throne, Jerusalem was finally destroyed and the rule of David's line came to an end.

It might be suggested that the fall of the Davidic kingship was only an interlude, an interruption, and that the kingdom of David would be restored at some future date. But the idea of *forever* clearly implies unbroken succession. It would not be very reassuring to think that the promise that you will live forever might involve an interruption of several thousand years along the way.

The resolution of this problem may be found in the typological role of the old-covenant king and his kingdom. A type is a kind of illustration, and any illustration inevitably contains imperfections — otherwise the illustration itself would be the thing being illustrated. So a king depicting the future role of Jesus the Christ invariably will possess imperfections in his rule that will never be found in the real thing. All prophetic shadows of the old covenant contain less of the reality of redemption than what is found in the new-covenant substance.

Parallels in other shadowy forms of the old covenant may be helpful. The manna eventually ceased although God's feeding of his people goes on forever. Bloody sacrifices ceased although God's people still offer the perpetual sacrifice of praise to God. So the Davidic line ceased although Jesus Christ reigns forever as a descendant of David.

The typological role of David's throne is clearly seen when it is stated that Solomon in succeeding David "sat on the throne of the LORD as king in place of his father David" (1 Chron. 29:23). Solomon sat on the Lord's throne! Obviously Solomon was not actually sitting in heaven on the throne of God in a material sense. Instead he was sitting on a figure — a shadowy image of the throne of God. Since David's throne was meant to depict God's own throne, the significance of the locale of this old-covenant throne imagery becomes plain. Both David's throne and God's are located in the same place.

Jesus Christ the Messiah of David now sits on God's throne, which is David's throne. He rules in heaven from the right hand of God, the new-covenant fulfillment of the old-covenant shadow. The promise of an eternal rule by David's divine Son finds its fulfillment in the rule of Christ from the right hand of God the Father. That rule has already begun. The promise that it will last eternally means that the rule of Jesus Christ will never be interrupted — not for a moment, not for an hour.

Kings and Queens for God

Every participant in the new covenant has a personal stake in this sonship established by God's covenant with David. Each believer also is viewed by God as a king. Accordingly Paul applies to every believer this very verse about the descendant of David:

> Come out from them and be separate . . . . I will be a father to you [plural], and you [plural] will be my sons and daughters (2 Cor. 6:17, 18).

Indeed Jesus Christ is the Son of God in a unique sense. He is the "radiance of God's glory and the exact representation of his being, sustaining all things by his powerful word" (Heb. 1:3). He is the fullest realization of the prophecy about David's descendant being God's royal son (cf Heb. 1:5). Yet this covenant of the kingdom made with David also speaks directly about *every* believer as God's royal son or daughter. By faith in Jesus Christ a man or a woman becomes heir and ruler in God's kingdom.

Take comfort! Nothing will ever interrupt the sovereign rule of your priestly King, the Lord Jesus Christ. He will always order the events of the world, whether small or great, for the good of his people and for his own glory. As the poet has said:

> Trembling soul, beset by fears,
> "Thy God reigneth!"
> Look above and dry thy tears:
> "Thy God reigneth!"
> Though thy foes with pow'r assail,
> Naught against thee shall prevail;

Trust in him—he'll never fail:
  "Thy God reigneth,
  Thy God reigneth!"

—Fred S. Shepherd

Review Questions

1. What three events set the stage for David's kingdom?

2. What are the two major emphases of the Davidic covenant?

3. How is God's promise to David of eternal rule being fulfilled today?

Discussion Questions

1. How are participants in the new covenant children of God as David was in his day? In other words, is God our Father in the same sense as he was David's or in a different sense?

2. Choose one of your favorite psalms, perhaps one that has been especially helpful to you in the past few weeks. Rephrase the psalm in your own words. You might wish to indicate how Christ fulfills the role of God in the psalm and how the psalm relates personally to you. For example, if Psalm 144 was an encouragement to you, you might paraphrase verses 3 and 4 this way:

   > LORD Christ, who is Nancy that you care for her,
   >   the daughter of a human that you think of her?
   > She is like a breath;
   >   her days are like a fleeting shadow.

3. How does the concept of Christ's now being seated on David's throne in heaven affect expectations about a future reign of Christ from a throne located in Palestine? Would a location of his throne in a single geographical location represent advancement or retrogression in relation to his present situation?

11

THE CONSUMMATION OF IT ALL

Christ: The Covenant of Consummation (I)

The promises of the new covenant are great; but are they for you? Are they being fulfilled in this age? Look at just a sampling of passages from the new-covenant Scriptures for an answer to that question.

> Luke 22:20: This cup is the new covenant in my blood, which is poured out for you.

> Hebrews 10:15-17 (quoting Jeremiah's "new-covenant" prophecy): The Holy Spirit also testifies to us about this. First he says: "This is the covenant I will make with them . . . . I will put my laws in their hearts." Then he adds, "Their sins and lawless acts I will remember no more."

> 1 John 2:27: As for you, the anointing you received from him remains in you, and you do not need anyone to teach you (cf Jer. 31:34).

There you have it—three different authors of the New Testament apply central aspects of the new covenant to the present day! Every time you celebrate the Lord's Supper you are participating in one of its principle blessings. According to the writer to the Hebrews it is to *us* that the prophecy of the forgiveness of sins was written. In the apostle John's understanding, the anointing of God's Holy

Spirit that gives immediate spiritual perception is a present reality. You who believe in Christ don't have to wait to know the fullness of life that comes through the outpouring of God's Holy Spirit on you.

A New Covenant

Because of your personal involvement in the blessings of the new covenant, consider the substance of the original old-covenant prophecy that depicts the future in covenantal terms. The Lord's prophets depicted the future in terms of a covenant. They say that the long-term future of mankind will be determined by a covenantal structure. This fact underscores the continuing importance of God's covenant.

Jeremiah is the one prophet who uses the phrase *new covenant*. He does so only in one passage (Jer. 31:31-34), although numerous other places in Jeremiah and his contemporary Ezekiel develop the same idea (Jer. 32:37-41; 50:4, 5; Ezek. 37:24-28; 16:60-63; 34).

A Covenantal Slide Show

From the prophecies just mentioned, several emphases related to the new covenant may be noted. First, this "new covenant" will be accompanied by the return of exiled Israel to the land. Exile represented a massive reversal of God's blessing under the old covenant. Israel was cast out of its land. But under the new covenant the people of God will be restored to their land. The new covenant will realize God's original promises given to Abraham and even to Adam concerning the possession of paradise.

What does this promise mean to you today? What is the cash value of the promise of the land? One-dollar bills printed by the United States mint used to include the phrase "silver certificate." That phrase meant that one dollar's worth of actual silver could be demanded at any federal bank in exchange for a one-dollar bill. What is the exchange value of the promise of the land?

Some would say that the exchange value is zero unless you happen to be Jewish, even though the New Testament says that every Christian believer is an inheritor of the promises of the new covenant. Others would say that the exchange value of this promise would be a portion of the physical land of Palestine someday in the future. Yet it seems rather bizarre to imagine all Christians and believing Jews who have lived over the centuries trying to share the little land of Palestine.

A better answer to this question may be found by seeing the imagery of the land promised to Abraham as a photographic slide. It is a picture taken of the paradise God originally established for Adam and Eve projected into the future as a land flowing with milk and honey. The promise of Palestine was a little picture of paradise restored.

When this picture is projected by the prophets into the future it expands once more to its original size in paradise. The land appears as a transformed heaven and earth. The whole cosmos receives renewal. The paradise of creation, having shrunk for a time to the pictorial dimensions of Palestine, finally expands once more in terms of the new heavens and the new earth.

This concept may be depicted graphically:

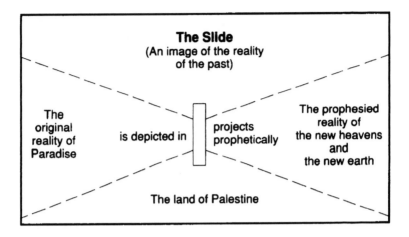

When the new-covenant prophecies refer to the promise of the land, think back to the original reality of the land of paradise from which the slide was made. Then project into the future in terms of the new heavens and the new earth. As a modern-day participant in the new covenant you are an heir to the new world promised by God.

According to the vision of John, the new Jerusalem associated with the new heavens and the new earth will measure 1500 miles in length, width and height (Rev. 21:16). Its inhabitants will be a multitude of peoples that no one can number. With the possibility of literally billions of square miles of surface space, this consummation-city could not fit into Palestine, which measures only about forty miles wide in the vicinity of Jerusalem. The new heavens, the new earth and the new Jerusalem break the bonds of the old typological city.

As a member by faith of the Israel of God you may look forward to your restoration to the land God has promised.

The new heavens, the new earth and the new Jerusalem are your habitation for eternity.

The Blessed Land

A second promise of the new covenant is the full restoration of blessings on the land. The desert will bloom and every man will reside in peace under his own vine and his own fig tree. This promise of restored blessing on the land and its inhabitants finds a dramatic depiction in Ezekiel's vision of the dry bones (Ezek. 37:1-14). Ezekiel sees a valley of very dry bones. He is told to prophesy to the bones. Before his eyes the bones come alive, are covered with sinews and flesh and receive the breath of life. In interpreting this vision the Lord says, "I am going to open your graves . . . I will bring you back to the land of Israel" (Ezek. 37:12). This promise is identified as a part of the everlasting covenant, the covenant of peace (Ezek. 37:26).

This same connection between the restoration of the land and the resurrection of the dead is found in Paul's description of the age of the Spirit. Paul declares that the whole creation has been groaning as in the pains of childbirth even as we ourselves "wait eagerly for . . . the redemption of our bodies" (Rom. 8:22, 23). We today as participants of the new covenant expect a new heaven and a new earth in which we in our resurrection bodies will enjoy the full restoration of blessings on the land.

Life at the Final Stage

Third, the new covenant promises the fulfillment of all the previous covenant commitments of the Lord. In this same section of Ezekiel the prophet combines the charac--

teristics of the Davidic, the Mosaic and the Abrahamic covenants and indicates that they will all reach fulfillment with the everlasting covenant of peace. God's servant will reign (Davidic); God's people will keep his laws and decrees (Mosaic); they will live in the land given to Jacob (Abrahamic — see Ezek. 37:24-28). The new covenant is not new in the sense that it is novel: it involves the consummation of all the previous promises of God.

Fourth, the new covenant will renew the heart. God promises this change of the inner man as a guarantee that the blessings of the covenant will be experienced: ʼ

> I will give you a new heart and put a new spirit in you; I will remove from you your heart of stone and give you a heart of flesh. And I will put my Spirit in you and move you to follow my decrees and be careful to keep my laws (Ezek. 36:26, 27).

This same promise undergirds Jeremiah's prophecy concerning the new covenant. The new heart and the possession of God's Spirit is a glorious promise that the Lord is now fulfilling in this age of the new covenant.

Fifth, full forgiveness of sins comes with the new covenant. This pardon is the foundation of the new covenant (Jer. 31:34). Because all sins are forgiven the blessings of the covenant can be experienced. A search will be made for the iniquity of Israel but no sin will be found (Jer. 50:20). God will cleanse them of their iniquities, pardoning them fully (Jer. 33:8).

Is not that forgiveness the joy of the believer in Christ today? Cannot the one who trusts in his death for their sins identify himself as one who shares in the blessedness of God's new-covenant people?

Sixth, the reunion of Israel and Judah is also involved in the blessings of the new covenant. Israel will come together with the sons of Judah, seeking the Lord (Jer. 50:4). One Shepherd-King of the Davidic line will rule over the reunited nation (Ezek. 34:23).

These words about the unity of God's people under the new covenant remind us of strikingly similar words of Jesus. He said, "I have other sheep that are not of this sheep pen. . . . They too will listen to my voice, and there shall be one flock and one shepherd" (John 10:16, 17). Jesus Christ, the Good Shepherd who lays down his life for the sheep, unites in himself all the various sheep into a single fold.

Not only does he unite believing Israelites of various origins, he also unites gentile believers with them. The other sheep who are not Israelites will come from the gentile nations. These other sheep are gathered into a single fold under Jesus. Practically speaking, this teaching means that there should be no "Messianic Jews" organized as a church in isolation from believing Gentiles. Instead there should be one flock with Christ as the single Shepherd.

The apostle Paul speaks directly of this same blessing of the new covenant. He describes it as a mystery once concealed but now revealed (Eph. 3:2-5). The mystery is that through the gospel the Gentiles are heirs together with Israel, members together of one body and sharers together in the promise of Christ Jesus (Eph. 3:6).

Heirs together, members together, sharers together — Gentiles inherit exactly the same promises along with Jewish believers. Whatever belongs by promise to Israel of the old covenant now belongs to Gentiles of the new covenant. Both groups are enriched beyond measure by sharing together these promises of God. That is the blessing of the new covenant.

Seventh, permanency is an essential characteristic of the new covenant. Although aspects of the previous covenants of God had everlasting dimensions, the new covenant is unique. It is unique in that in its wholeness it is everlasting — everything in it is forever. There are stages in its realization but it will not be supplemented or supplanted by a subsequent covenantal relationship.

In a distinctive sense the new covenant is the last covenant. Because it will accomplish that which God has intended all along in redemption, it will never be superseded by a subsequent covenant.

What a privilege it is to live today! *You* can be a participant in God's last great covenant. The fullness of time has come. The future age that the prophets saw is being realized. It is your joy to share in the rich blessings of the new-covenant age.

Review Questions

1. List seven emphases in the Old Testament prophets' depiction of the new covenant.

2. How is the imagery of the land in Old Testament literature like a photographic slide?

Discussion Questions

1. How is your own home a picture of what God has promised to give you eternally?

2. Choose one of the seven emphases from Review Question 1 and apply it to your marriage or to your work responsibilities. How does this prophetic promise undergird your efforts and encourage you? What prayer requests does it suggest to you?

12

FINDING THE BALANCE

Christ: The Covenant of Consummation (II)

A seesaw can be lots of fun — if the seesaw is kept in balance. But if someone overenthusiastic gets wound up on one end he can make life miserable for the person on the other.

The new covenant is intended to be a blessing for all its participants, but truth about the new covenant must be kept in balance. If a person goes too far in the direction of any of the various aspects of the new covenant it will create serious problems. Notice these areas in which finding the balance is essential to the proper enjoyment of all the blessings of the new covenant.

Everything Old Has Become New

Balance must be found between continuity and newness in the relation of the old covenant to the new. This last covenant is a new covenant. All the freshness, the surprise, the exhilaration of a new toy or a new machine characterizes the covenant under which you live today. But the new covenant is also attached to the old. It represents continuity with the past as well as newness for the present. Jeremiah's prophecy says that the day of a new covenant is coming. This new covenant will not be like the old covenant God made with the forefathers (Jer. 31:31, 32).

With which covenant of old does the new covenant contrast? Obviously it stands over against the Mosaic covenant of law. But that is not the full picture of the contrast, as Jeremiah's prophecy indicates. This new covenant will contrast with the old covenant "when I took them by the hand to lead them out of Egypt" (Jer. 31:32). At the time of God's leading the people out of Egypt the Mosaic covenant was not in effect. Israel was delivered out of Egypt under the provisions of the Abrahamic covenant (see Ex. 6:4-6). Furthermore Jeremiah himself lived in the days of the Davidic covenant. When he prophesied about a new covenant coming in the future he spoke about a covenant that would stand in contrast with the Davidic covenant of his own day as well. The new covenant contrasts with the Mosaic, the Davidic and the Abrahamic covenants of old. It is indeed a radically new thing, unknown previously in human history.

The drastic contrast is dramatized by Jeremiah's declaration that this new covenant came into existence because Israel had broken the old covenant (Jer. 31:32). The phrase *because they broke my covenant* actually declares that Israel had nullified the old covenant. In one sense the break between the old and the new covenants is so great that it may be said that the old covenant came to an end with the arrival of the new covenant.

For this reason the new covenant must not be seen merely as a renewal of the old covenant. The Qumran community of Jesus' day understood the new covenant in this erroneous way. They expected a reinstatement of the old Mosaic laws as the sign of the arrival of the new covenant. Some current thinking about the new covenant moves along similar lines. Some Christians expect in the near future a kingdom that will last for a thousand years in which the old Mosaic laws about sacrifice will be reinstituted.

But the newness of the new covenant must be appreciated more fully. That old covenant is nullified, cancelled and set aside. It is replaced by the new. At the same time, a balance must be kept. As the summation of all God's covenant dealings with fallen men the new covenant remains connected with the old.

One point of continuity is found in the reference to the Torah, the law that God will write in the hearts of new-covenant participants. "I will write my Torah on their hearts," says the Lord (Jer. 31:33). In essence it is the same law of the old covenant that is now written on the hearts of new-covenant participants. Not all the details of the ceremonial and civil laws may apply, for they were attached to the peculiar form of the constitution of old-covenant Israel. But the essence of God's Torah, the abiding law of the Ten Commandments, is now written in the hearts of men and women. A solid line of continuity in the covenants is established.

A further point of continuity between the old covenant and the new is seen in the fact that the new covenant completes the redemption promised under the old. "I was a husband to them," says the Lord in describing his relation to Israel under the old covenant (Jer. 31:32). All the tender care and affection that Christ expresses to his bride, the church, was present in the redemptive love of God to Israel under the old covenant. Completing this redemptive love by Christ binds the covenants, old and new, to one another.

The centrality of forgiveness in the covenants also binds old and new together. Many sacrifices symbolized forgiveness in the old covenant. In the new God promises that he will "remember . . . no more" the sins of his people (Jer. 31:34). Count your blessings, and number the forgiveness of sins at the top of the list. You can see the continuity with the past by the centrality of the old-covenant sacrificial system. But Jeremiah places the experience of the new-covenant believer in another realm: no remembrance of sins! Even as the old-covenant believer sacrificed for sin, his very actions in seeking forgiveness involved a remembrance of sin. But no more sacrifices are required under the new covenant. Once and for all the final sacrifice has been offered. To share in the freedom from remembrance of sin is one of the great blessings of the new covenant.

The One and the Many

Balance must also be found between corporateness and individuality in the relation of the old covenant to the new. At times it has been proposed that the uniqueness of the new covenant is found in its stress on the role of the individual in determining his personal relation to God. This stress on individualism contrasts with the emphasis on corporateness in the old covenant. One modern commentator summarizes this position in the following manner:

> In acclaiming this new form of covenantal relationship Jeremiah and Ezekiel saw that it changed the

older concept of a corporate relationship completely by substituting the individual for the nation as a whole.

Probably the most significant contribution which Jeremiah made to religious thought was inherent in his insistence that the new covenant involved a one-to-one relationship to the Spirit. When the new covenant was inaugurated by the atoning work of Jesus Christ on Calvary, this important development of personal, as opposed to corporate, faith and spirituality was made real for the whole of mankind. (Harrison, R. K. *Jeremiah and Lamentations.* Downers Grove, Ill., 1973: 140.)

This perspective suggests a total discontinuity in the aspect of the old covenant and the new. The new covenant is understood as having completely changed the old by substituting *individual* for *corporate* relationships. The personal faith and spirituality of the new covenant is presented as being diametrically opposed to the corporate faith and spirituality of the old covenant.

However, the matter is not quite so simple. Were not the old-covenant people responsible to manifest personal and individual faith? Yes they were. At the same time, the words of Jeremiah actually say that the new covenant will be made with the house of Israel and with the house of Judah (Jer. 31:31, 33). This language hardly suggests a substitution of individualism in place of corporate relationships in the new covenant.

A heightening of *both* these dimensions may be seen in the new covenant. The apostle John interprets the prophetic utterance of Caiaphas concerning one man's death for the nation:

[H]e prophesied that Jesus would die for the Jewish nation, and not only for that nation but also for the scattered children of God, to bring them together and make them one (John 11:51, 52).

Each individual is responsible for embracing the Savior by his own personal faith, but in the new covenant God continues to deal corporately. The Lord administers the grace of the new covenant with households and with the church as a whole. "The house of Judah" or " . . . of Israel" ultimately refers to the elect people of God. It is with these people as a unit that the new covenant is established.

A tension may well exist between the corporate body of the church and the individuals who are saved by the grace of God. Not all those in the visible church may be saved. But this fact must not lead to discounting the corporate body as the framework of God's dealing with his people. The balance must be established between the corporate and the individual dimensions of the new covenant. Each has its role to play.

Within and Without

Balance must be found between internal reality and external form in the blessings of the new covenant. Stress clearly falls on internal realities in the new covenant. God promises that he will write his law in their hearts (Jer. 31:33). If the old covenant had the law written on stone tablets external to mankind, the new covenant has the same law inscribed within the heart. But does this contrast mean that there was no renewing of the heart under the old covenant? Was there no indwelling of the Holy Spirit for the old-covenant believer?

A number of verses in the old covenant answer this question by describing the saving effect of the Spirit's work in the heart of the old-covenant believer (cf Deut. 6:6; 11:18; 10:12, 16; 30:6, 14; Ps. 37:31; 40:8; 51:12, 19; 73:1,13; Is. 51:7; Jer. 4:4,14; 9:25; 23:9). How could it be that anyone could be saved apart from the regenerating work of the Holy Spirit? How could the renewed life of the old-covenant believer be sustained apart from the work of the life-giving Spirit of God?

At the same time, the new-covenant believer *does* experience the Spirit of God in a way not fully understood by the people of the old covenant. Three distinctives of the experiences of the Spirit under the new covenant may be noted.

1. The fullness of the Holy Spirit by which he permeates the whole of life finds a fuller realization under the new covenant. Because of the fuller revelation of Christ the new-covenant believer may expect permeation of the Spirit's influence throughout his life.

2. The special gifts of the Spirit that make possible the ministry of one believer to another find a greater manifestation under the new covenant. God promised through Joel that he would pour out his Spirit on all flesh. All believers under the new covenant share in the richness of these gifts.

3. The ministry of God's Spirit now comes immediately (i.e., without mediator) from the resurrected Christ who is seated in glory at the right hand of the Father's power. By Christ's resurrection a new historical era has been introduced in which God's people are taught more immedi-

ately by Christ in his glory. Having been anointed of the Spirit himself he is in a position to pour out his Spirit on all flesh.

The origin of the office of teacher in the old covenant goes back to the time of Moses. At Mount Sinai the people were terrified. They wanted a mediator, a teacher (*moreh*) to communicate the truth of God to them. This arrangement under the old covenant solved the immediate problem felt by the people. They could receive God's word without direct contact with him. But a mediator contradicts the very essence of the covenant itself. The goal of God in the covenant of redemption was to create oneness between himself and his people. So long as a mediator exists between God and his people the oneness intended by the covenant cannot be fully realized.

The great blessing of the new covenant comes with the termination of any need for covenantal mediators. *All* shall know the Lord immediately. Without any need for a go-between, men can know him firsthand. From the least to the greatest, all shall have a personal acquaintance with him.

According to the appointment of God, the new covenant has not yet been realized to its fullest degree. In the present time teachers raised up with the gifts of the Spirit will continue to instruct God's people, but the day will soon come in which the complete unity of God with his people will be realized. Then the only teacher will be the Lord himself.

The internal realities of God's relation to his people are stressed in the new covenant. By the greater experience of the Spirit's dwelling within every believer, the fuller blessings of the new covenant are realized. Yet at the same time, the external blessings of God's people are not ignored in the new covenant. God's ordering of the material world for the good of his people includes provision of all things necessary for life and godliness. Ultimately the blessings of the new heavens and the new earth will be inherited by every participant in the new covenant. By the resurrection of the body which will occur through the Spirit the final blessing of the Lord of the covenant will be poured out on his people.

In the end, all the promises of the ancient covenants of God with his people find their fulfillment in the new covenant. For Christ is the All in All, the beginning and the end, the Alpha and the Omega, the consummation of God's covenants. To him be the glory for ever and ever. Amen.

Review Questions

1. What are the areas in which finding the proper balance is essential to enjoyment of the new covenant?

2. What makes it especially difficult for you to balance your internal experiences of the grace of God with the external?

Discussion Questions

1. How does our fondness for new things make it difficult for us to appreciate the continuity of the old covenant into the new?

2. Agree or disagree: "The American pioneer spirit of rugged individualism undermines corporate responsibility in the church."

3. How would you prove that the Holy Spirit was at work in believers during the old covenant?

13

THE CROSS AND THE COVENANT

All roads lead to Rome, right? Wrong! Two thousand years ago the myth was exploded: all roads do *not* lead to Rome. Instead all roads lead to the cross. All the roads of time, all the roads of history, all the avenues of man's successes and failures in the world lead to the cross of our Lord Jesus Christ.

The word *cross* is related directly to the words *crux, crisis* and *critical*. The cross is the critical center of all things past, present and future.

To understand all its fullness the cross must be seen from the perspective of the covenant. The covenant illuminates the cross; the covenant magnifies the cross; the covenant highlights the majesty and might of the cross of our Lord Jesus Christ.

Why the Cross?

One of the older saints of the church wrote a little book entitled *Cur Deus Homo?* or *Why Did God Become Man?* In this book Anselm wrestled with a profound question: Why did Jesus Christ have to die? Wouldn't it have been possible for God to forgive men's sins apart from the terribleness of the death of our Lord Jesus Christ? As you read this ancient little treatise you can see significant contributions made by Anselm toward an answer to this question, although all his reasoning may not be convincing. Anselm begins by stating that God had to become man in order to maintain his own glory as God. If man remained in a fallen condition God's honor would be damaged.

The apostle Paul would appear to disagree with Anselm on this point, for according to Paul God is glorified even when he brings righteous judgment on the wicked (Rom. 9:22). It wasn't necessary for God to save sinners so that his honor might be maintained. God could have been glorified by his bringing a just and righteous judgment on the wicked.

In another argument this old theologian struck closer to the heart of the matter. Why did Christ have to die? Theologians have called this second answer of Anselm the "antecedent absolute necessity" of the atonement. The word *antecedent* refers to something that goes before. Anselm argues that something went before the absolute necessity of the death of our Lord Jesus Christ. What is that antecedent? It was God's commitment in the covenant to save sinful men and women.

Once God had committed himself to save sinners, only one way was possible for this intent to become reality: God's Son, the Lord Jesus Christ, would have to die in the place of sinners. If God would be just and the justifier of the ungodly, he would have to sacrifice his own Son to suffer the righteous judgment that sin deserves. The antecedent absolute necessity of the atonement refers to this commitment on God's part to redeem sinners even at the cost of his own Son. Even though salvation could come only through a righteous substitutionary sacrifice for sins, the Lord of heaven and earth did not hold back his only Son.

This solemn commitment of the Lord is embedded in the concept of the covenant as a "bond in blood sovereignly administered." Because of sin that violated man's commitment in the covenant, a death had to occur to accomplish redemption. That death came to pass in the cross of our Lord Jesus Christ. In every phase of the covenant of redemption the cross of Christ is central. The wonders and the glories of the mighty cross of Christ are to be perceived from the perspective of the entire flow of human history.

The Cross in the Garden

The words to the serpent in the garden join cross and covenant. Satan might wound with a mighty blow the Savior born of woman, but in striking his crushing blow Satan himself would receive a deadly blow to the head. Jesus ultimately made an open display of his triumph over satanic powers in his cross (Col. 2:14, 15). Every injustice in the world committed by the powers of government, business or society derives its inspiration from Satan. Yet the cross of Jesus Christ has broken the strength of those powers.

The Cross at the Flood

The covenant that God made with Noah also centers on the cross of Christ. The flood anticipates the judgment that God ultimately would bring on his own Son, the Lord Jesus Christ. Our Lord spoke as the drowning sinner when he cried: "My God, why hast thou forsaken me?" By suffering death Christ fulfilled the commitments God made in the covenant with Noah. God the righteous Judge could preserve the earth filled with wickedness only by providing a substitute for the sinner. It was in anticipation of the Lord Jesus Christ's receiving the judgment due sinners that salvation was provided for Noah and his family.

The Cross on the Mountain

Next comes the covenant with Abraham. Once more the cross of Christ is central. God said to Abraham, "Take your son, your only son, Isaac, whom you love, and go to the region of Moriah. Sacrifice him there as a burnt offering on one of the mountains I will tell you about" (Gen. 22:2). How wonderful was the faith of Abraham! He said to his servants, "Stay here with the donkey while I and the boy go over there. *We* will worship and *we* will come back to you" (Gen. 22:5—emphasis added). The writer to the Hebrews says that Abraham had faith that if necessary God would raise Isaac from the dead (Heb. 11:19).

Consider the problem from Abraham's perspective. He knew that God could not lie. He knew that God had designated Isaac as the one through whom the seed of promise must come. Yet he also received God's command that he must sacrifice his son Isaac. Apart from faith it would appear that God clearly had contradicted himself, but by faith Abraham concluded that if necessary God would raise his son from the dead.

Abraham was to offer his son on Mount Moriah. The centrality of the cross emerges with the mention of Moriah in a later incident of the Old Testament. In this later day, David sees the angel of the Lord with his sword drawn against Jerusalem. Because of David's sin God's judgment hovers over the city (see 1 Chron. 21). David approaches Araunah the Jebusite with the intent of purchasing a place for sacrifice. Araunah offers to donate land, cattle and whatever else might be necessary for the king's offering, but David insists that he will not present to the Lord something that costs him nothing. He buys the land and purchases his own sacrifices. David concludes that the house of the Lord must be located on this site. The altar of burnt offering must be at this place. The temple of God must stand here.

Do you see the connection of this incident with the offering of Isaac? With the cross of Christ? Not quite yet — not until you note that Solomon later built the temple of the Lord in Jerusalem on Mount Moriah where the Lord had appeared to his father David. Solomon built his temple on the site of the threshing floor of Araunah the Jebusite (2 Chron. 3:1), precisely where Abraham had offered Isaac a thousand years before David!

Abraham journeys for three days to a mountain called Moriah, where he offers his son — his only son whom he loves. At this same place King David offers a sacrifice to deliver Jerusalem from the judgment of God. Solomon subsequently builds his great temple on this very site, and for a thousand years the sacrifices of the Jewish people are offered on Mount Moriah. To that place Jesus Christ came and presented himself as the Lamb of God that takes away the sin of the world. The sacrifice which Abraham was *willing* to make, God *made*.

What is the point of this connection of place? Is it to make holy that place where Muslims today have built their "dome of the rock"? Is this place holy according to current Jewish restrictions which forbid any Jew to enter the temple area because of the possibility of defiling the "most holy place"?

The connections of history point in another direction. All those old events of Scripture foreshadow the one reality of the offering of the Son of God. Not the *place* but the *person* is holy. The center of history, the center of God's covenant commitments, is to be found in the cross of Christ. The wonder is not to be found in the willingness of God's people to sacrifice to the Lord, but the commitment of the Lord to sacrifice for his people.

The Cross in the Wilderness

The covenant of Moses centers on this same theme. Moses lifted up the serpent in the wilderness as a sign that the serpent had been cursed. "Anyone who is hung on a tree is under God's curse," said the law of Moses (Deut. 21:23; cf Gal. 3:13). The tree had been created as a source of blessing to the world. It was designed to provide shade in summer and warmth in winter. Fruit and lumber came from the tree. But when man hangs dying on a tree the whole creational order has been turned upside down. Instead of being a blessing to man the tree becomes a curse.

The serpent lifted on a pole signifies the curse of the Tempter. God's people are shown, in a most startling manner, that they must look in faith to an object that has been cursed. A serpent on a pole is the way of their salvation.

How can this be? The truth of God must be handled delicately, but the principle is clear. God the Father looking down on his Son on the cross saw a cursed figure comparable to the serpent on the pole; for God "made [Christ] who had no sin to be sin for us, so that in him we might become the righteousness of God" (2 Cor. 5:21). All the ugliness of sin was heaped on the Lord Jesus Christ as he hung on the cross. He did not himself sin but sin was imputed to him.

As you look in faith to that cursed one hanging on a tree, all of the curses due to you for your sin will be forever removed. You will be healed from the curse of death even as was Israel in the wilderness. The righteous requirement of the law of Moses regarding the punishment of sinners finds its fulfillment in the covenant death of our Lord Jesus Christ.

The Cross and the King

The cross is central also in the Davidic covenant. Through God's bond with David it becomes apparent that even in the daily walk of the Christian the cross and the covenant provide the key. These two elements—cross and covenant —cannot be separated from one another.

One of the most striking dimensions of the life of King David is found in the chastening he receives from the hand of the Lord. When God entered into covenant with him he was told that if he and his sons walked according to God's commandments the Lord would bless their line and their rule. But if they disobeyed he would chasten them with the rod of men and with the stripes of men (2 Sam. 7:14).

Now David, the man after God's own heart, falls into an awful sin: he commits adultery and murder. After a year of hardening his heart against the conviction of the Holy Spirit David is confronted by Nathan the prophet. The king's heart is broken: "I have sinned against the Lord," he confesses. Nathan responds, "The Lord has forgiven your sin. But you will suffer discipline from the chastening hand of God."

In accord with the provisions of God's covenant, David receives the blessing of forgiveness along with chastening from the Lord. Even though a king, he will be disciplined for his sin through the rest of his life. Yet throughout those many years of tragedy and suffering he is able to write psalm after psalm praising and thanking God.

How is this possible? It is because David knows his chastening to be a sign of God's covenant faithfulness to him. Even these hardest of times will serve to bless "the man after God's own heart."

Because covenant and cross are bound together, you can live every day with absolute confidence that whatever comes into your life originates from the loving hand of your Father. He has bound himself in love through the bond of the covenant in the cross of our Lord Jesus Christ.

The Perfections of the Cross

All the old-covenant shadows come to consummate realization in the cross of the new covenant. The perfections of the cross of our Lord Jesus Christ bring the long history of covenant administration to its final fulfillment. For this reason the cross of Christ must be the center of your entire life. Listen to Paul as he affirms the centrality of the cross: "I have been crucified with Christ and I no longer live, but Christ lives in me. The life I live in the body, I live by faith in the Son of God, who loved me and gave himself for me" (Gal. 2:20).

Since the cross serves as the center of history there can be no other focus for your life. You in your turn must take up your cross. You must die to yourself. Your only reason for living must be found in union with Christ in his cross. As you in faith set your gaze on him, all the promises of God's covenants become yours. You may live in the wonder of the fact that you are bound in covenant relation with God just as firmly as was Adam, Noah, Abraham, Moses and David. Through the love of Christ for sinners as seen in the cross, by faith you are his and he is yours. "May I never boast except in the cross of our Lord Jesus Christ, through which the world has been crucified to me, and I to the world" (Gal. 6:14).

Review Questions

1. Why did Christ have to die? Couldn't God simply have forgiven man's sins?

2. List the ways that the cross of Christ is central in each phase of the covenant of redemption.

3. Write out three ways your practice in either your marriage or your work has changed for the better as a result of the study of God's covenants.

Discussion Questions

1. How do the injustices committed by governments in the world today reflect the pattern of Satan in the garden (i.e., lying, denying God's commands, exaggeration, etc.)? Which of these injustices seems most Satanic to you? How does the pattern of Christ's passion contradict Satan's way?

2. How does Christ's death provide a rationale for the preservation of the earth? Does this mean simply that Christians should be better environmentalists than are the secularists?

3. How does Moses's lifting up the serpent in the wilderness help you understand the significance of forgiveness through Christ's blood? Read aloud 2 Corinthians 5:21 and meditate on it as an explanation of the centrality of the cross. How can these truths help you deal with a particular sense of guilt right now?